SEEING BEHIND THE *Mask*

Spiritual Discernment
For The Days Ahead

SEEING BEHIND THE *Mask*

Spiritual Discernment
For The Days Ahead

By

DIANE EHRLICH

Reform Ministry Publications

ISBN: 1460949900
ISBN-13: 978-1460949900

Published by Reform Ministry Publications
Cleveland, Ohio
www.reformministry.com

My Prayer

And this is my prayer: that your love may abound more and more in knowledge and insight, so that you may be able to discern what is best…to the glory and praise of God.

Philippians 1: 9-11

Contents

Forward

n July of 1999 I had the extreme privilege of hearing Josh McDowell of Campus Crusade for Christ give a lecture on "Personal Truth." He presented data verifying that people in America, especially young people, were rejecting biblical truth such as The Ten Commandments and opting for "personal truth" or "what is true for me." This cultural trend of relativism was something entirely new to me.

Later while reading my Bible, the Lord showed me 2 Thessalonians 2:11. **"For this reason God sends them a powerful delusion so that they will believe the lie and so that all will be condemned who have not believed the truth but have delighted in wickedness."** With one sentence from scripture, God explained the social trend that Josh referred to in his hour long speech. Such is the nature of real truth, which is biblical truth. It defines expansive topics, inviting the reader to look into the matter and discover more. That is exactly what I did.

Those events triggered my study of the New Testament warnings to beware of false teaching. Spiritual messages opposing the Gospel and confusing early believers were a prime concern for early church leaders. In light of cultural relativism, we should have the same concern today.

The thought of a massive wave of spiritual deception sweeping people up into accepting a lie was very disturbing to me. In order to sound a qualified alarm, I had to identify and then describe the common elements of today's false teachings. This called for much discernment. Although I don't claim to present a comprehensive account, I have tried to spot the representative divergent messages and then follow them out to show how severely they contradict God's Word.

My motive for writing this book was to convince people to return to a biblical world view that holds the Bible completely true and forsake competing cultural trends. Bible in hand, people can learn to engage in a vital relationship with God through Jesus Christ and remain in the truth. My heartfelt prayer is that readers will ask God for discernment in these matters so as to avoid the powerful oncoming delusion that scripture forewarns of and be able to know what is best to the glory of God.

Diane Ehrlich, Director
Reform Ministry
Cleveland, Ohio, 2011

Acknowledgements

I want to extend my utter gratitude to my prayer partners for believing in the value of this work and seeking God on my behalf. They are: Marilyn Woods, Tami Pepin, Shirley Barton, Diane Office and Sylvia Meder. Special thanks goes to Marilyn Woods, Cathy Monnin and Shirley Barton for proofreading and evaluating the early manuscript. Thank you for your important comments and corrections that gave this work its finishing touch.

Seeing Behind The Mask

INTRODUCTION

William Shakespeare once wrote "All the world's a stage, and all the men and women are merely players…"[1] Was this famous reflection merely poetic or timelessly prophetic? Is it possible that the unfolding drama of human events played out upon the planet could be likened to a theater of sorts? Can our world view, which is the way we see life, be condensed in such a way to consider a central idea of such enormity and reduce it down to a single summarization that accurately encompasses all that we see? Can this opening statement, in fact, be true?

Amazingly, yes! In the context of the biblical world view, which is the realty that is framed by the words of the Bible, the world can be likened to a stage. The drama of Deity, angels, devils, people, places and events that the Bible describes are all valid,

---

1 *As You Like It,* Shakespeare

real and true. The Bible is the exclusive Word of God given to man to reveal God's character and His involvement with us as we experience our individual segment of living. From that premise, we ascertain that it stands as the absolute standard of truth and is set apart as the Truth. **"...Your word is truth."** (John 17:17) Guided by truth, we can pursue the topic of world view within the vista of seeing the whole world as a stage.

Jesus said that when we know the truth, we are released from the consternation of doubt and mystery. **"If you abide in My word, then you are truly disciples of Mine; and you shall know the truth and the truth shall make you free."** (John 8:31-32) Awareness and clarity of ultimate fundamentals comprise the very nature of truth. It incorporates all the parameters, the pros and cons and discussions in between of grandiose subjects and reduces them down to bare basics to make them understandable with a single phrase. Truth unravels and resolves weighty questions and musings that keep us awake at night. The secret code is cracked, the riddle is solved and the light bulb in our head comes on as truth beams its way through the obscurity, allowing us to see the heart of the matter. It summarizes, simplifies and settles life's most voluminous issues. Rescued by truth, our mind stops racing and we can come to a place of resolve where we can rest and be quietly assured.

The objection may arise, "What does the individual gain from this task of so much thinking?" Examining our world view is actually a very important exercise because it brings us to a place where we know what we truly believe. Most of us don't really know. The majority of people are just guessing, hoping that they have it right with nothing firmly in place to anchor them.

All of our beliefs are based on underlying perspectives, values and basic assumptions about life in general. Unspoken ideas feed into us like an underground stream and we acquire them in a way that is more like absorption than understanding. Once ideas are in us, we become possessive of them. Like clothes in our closet that may not even fit, they become part of a collection that we cannot bear to toss out because they belong to us.

Identifying our operative world view may seem too deep to even express in words, yet our understanding at this level speaks to all that we see. Our system of beliefs controls us and our framework of ideas determines our behavior. Our private outlook will permeate our choices, color our preferences and launch all that we think, say and do. Therefore, we need to make a conscious effort to locate the premise by which we truly live. Christian philosopher Francis Schaeffer introduced his book *How Shall We Then Live?* this way, "People have presuppositions, and they will live more consistently on the basis of these presuppositions than they themselves may realize. By presuppositions we mean the basic way in which the individual looks at life, his basic world view, the grid through which he sees the world."[2]

Another reason why this inward decision process is so crucial is because our personal world would be rocked and shattered if we found out that, after our time of living thus far, our perspectives were based on falsehood. What a bitter pill to discover that we have wasted our years acting upon a lie. All of the ideas and definitions that we have grown accustomed to would collapse if the tide of truth rushed in and washed away the existing support system, like a house built upon the sand. This would be tragic because it would render all of our efforts as meaningless. Therefore, the pursuit of truth is not only beneficial but critical for the inner stability and outward success of the individual.

---

2 *How Shall We Then Live?* P. 19

Let me give an example of a faulty world view. At one time in human history, most people held the understanding that the earth was flat. They looked out across the horizon from man's vantage point and saw what they assumed was the end of terra firma. They feared that if they reached that edge, they would drop down into nothingness. This basic world view aroused much fear among sailors who expected to sail to a certain point and then fall to their death. According to one historical myth, people believed that the horizontal disc of the earth rested on the backs of four elephants that were balanced on top of a huge tortoise! Man's perspective evoked mythical explanations in order to resolve the vexing problem of the unknown.

That prevailing belief was proven wrong when a Christian man named Christopher Columbus dared to embrace what the Bible said about the earth. In the Book of Genesis, God's Word described the east and west of the ancient world. Combined with geography maps he obtained from China, Columbus knew that the world was a sphere. After Columbus successfully proved his theory by sailing to the New World, the rest of human civilization was forced to change their world view because of his discovery. Today, of course everyone knows that the earth is round, and the previously held world view and mythical explanations seem laughable. With this example in mind, we can zoom out beyond the flat scope of man's perspective to see the earth from God's vantage point. Looking down, we see the world as a stage and identify the players upon it participating in their different roles that the Bible describes.

Using the Bible as the standard of truth, my purpose for writing this book is to un-mask spiritual deception and to counter false teaching that leads people away from knowing God. The New Testament is loaded with warnings to stay free from erroneous teachings that undermine the simple message of the Gospel. Armed with spiritual discernment, we can see behind the mask of falsehood in order to identify and remove those ideas from our belief system.

We will explore topics such as the origin of supernatural evil, human sin nature, God's protective measures through the gift of discernment, how to spot modern modes of false teaching, and understanding the life saving choice to believe what God has told us. After reading, perhaps you will need to revamp your world view to see that this world is a stage and that we are merely players, but with sobering and significant parts to play. A new world of truth may appear that will comfort and fortify as you see behind the mask. I pray that you will take the time to review your beliefs to detect spiritual deception and choose to incorporate God's ways instead.

Biblical World View

CHAPTER ONE

The biblical world view begins with the belief that God created the heavens and the earth, and that He is separate and infinitely greater than His creation. **"In the beginning God created the heavens and the earth." (Genesis 1:1)** It also asserts that the occurrences described in Genesis Chapters 1, 2 and 3 are historical events rather than mere allegorical pictures. The depiction of a literal six day creation extravaganza to God's glory, the warning and subsequent disobedience of the first earthly couple, the entrance of sin that marred the whole creation and the mercy-filled promise of a world Savior are all packed into these first three chapters of the Bible. Physical death and the process of disease and dying are also introduced as part of the penalty of sin. By reading these chapters, we can answer the tough questions of the heart: How were things originally intended to be? What went wrong? How does this spiritual predicament affect us today and what can be done to avoid the harshness of it all?

The finality of death is the harshest reality that we have to deal with. We cannot deny death because we witness the beginning and end of things every day. A constant cycle of relationships, governments, and human lives come and go upon the planet. As participants in this cycle, we must admit that physical death for all living things is final. The Bible tells us, **"There is an appointed time for everything. And there is a time for every event under heaven—A time to give birth, and a time to die..."** **(Ecclesiastes 3:1-2)**

On a universal scale, people avoid or even refuse to talk about death because of the mystery that surrounds it. Death is inevitable and irreversible. The fear of death rattles our collective cage as mankind's most dreaded fear. Whether we realize it or not, the fear of facing our own mortality keeps us running in an effort to stay beyond its reach. As long as we can keep going, we trick ourselves into believing that we can escape its grasp.

Yet inside of us, a timid rational voice dares to ask the question, "But what happens after we die?" We may choose to ignore that voice in an attempt to escape its reality, but death will not ignore us. Some appointed day death will come to claim each of us and we will have no say in its arrest.

America's greatest dare devil, Evel Knievel, could not even defy death. He died in 2007 at age 69 after an extensive career in the entertainment industry of performing breathtaking motorcycle jumps. "After a wild ride of a life, a dare devil defies death no more," reported People Magazine in a tribute to his fame. [3] If Evel Knievel could not out-run nor out-jump death, then neither can we.

---

3 *People Magazine*, December 7, 2007

Some people see death as a cruel intruder, halting their eager plans in life. Others may see it as a welcome relief to end a life of bitter struggle. Regardless, just like those unenlightened sailors of old, the idea of suddenly falling off the edge of life into an unknown realm is unnerving if not terrifying. The Bible says that this fear captures the human heart in such a way that we can be emotionally paralyzed by it. When we face our own mortality, we must also admit our complete helplessness. Our inability to put this overwhelming fear into words renders this topic unspeakable. As a result, we may accept man-made myths and imaginary ideas to soothe our psyches and downplay its finality. Our speculation may seem to solve the mystery of death and we can temporarily still our deepest fear, but this can be the entrance point to spiritual deception.

Let's brave the unknown by looking at what the Bible says about death. Scripture deals with the topic of the hereafter quite openly and frequently. Within its pages, we can find the solution to relieve us from the paralysis of mental escapism. **"Since then the children share in flesh and blood, He Himself also partook of the same, that through death He might render powerless him who had the power of death, that is, the devil; and might deliver those who through fear of death were subject to slavery all their lives." (Hebrews 2: 14-15)** This passage tells us that Jesus, the Son of God, allowed Himself to experience death in His human body so that, by His resurrection from the dead, He would exert an even greater power over death on our behalf. This means that Jesus defeated death for us. Its power was overwhelmed by eternal life, which is the transporting of our soul into God's presence after we die. By uniting ourselves with Jesus, we can cross over and be delivered from the power of death to live safely with God forevermore.

Filled with this assurance, we are set free from the nagging fear of death and all the mystique that it entails. The veil of the unknown has been lifted by the acknowledgement of the work of Christ for us. We can know for sure that we will go to Heaven after we die because we have a living Christ to personally assure us. **"And the witness is this, that God has given us eternal life, and this life is in His Son. He who has the Son has life…" (1 John 5:11-12)** Knowing Jesus and having the eternal life that He provides gives us peace of mind that transcends the tentativeness of myths and suppositions about eternity.

If all the world is a stage, then the biblical world view names the key roles for the great drama that is being played out. Humanity is enslaved by the bondage to sin and the fear of death instilled by a devil who works to keep people deceived, distracted and disunited from their Heavenly Father. The Bible describes a Savior, Christ Jesus, who has personally defeated death and has the ability to rescue people from their immanent peril. We can identify an ongoing spiritual dual between a supernatural devil who hates us and a Divine Savior who loves us. When we embrace this perspective, then the blinders of sin and escapism come off, and we are released to a paradigm that suddenly makes sense. God welcomes all people to enter into the eternal rescue plan that He has provided through Jesus Christ. Simply by admitting our sin, we can turn away from it and accept the forgiveness that Christ has won. You can pray a prayer to do this at the end of the book.

THE PHANTOM OF THE OPERA

Permit me to describe this earthly drama in greater detail by using modern media to explain the players. I will use scenes from Andrew Lloyd Weber's musical "The Phantom of the Opera" to offer a visual resource to guide our mind's eye into understanding biblical truth. This play/movie has been viewed by millions of people around the world and stands as an allegory to the activity of the spirit realm, revealing the genius of spiritual deception. I will give an interpretation of this allegory in order to unmask the purveyor of a diabolical plot against mankind since the beginning of time. The supernatural evil of this scheme is unfathomable and seems too horrible to possibly be true. Yet, if we dare to see the world as a stage, then the glaring presence of the players of this cosmic battle comes forth and the dynamics of biblical world view emerges as convincing truth. Let's begin with scenes from the movie.

The heroine, Christine Deye, is a beautiful talented young opera student who was brought under the wing of the opera mistress after her father died. To comfort his daughter before his death, Christine's father promises to send the "angel of music" to continue teaching her after he is gone. She believes the fantasy promise and easily falls into a relationship with a "spirit" who speaks to her from the shadows, telling her that he is the "angel of music" that her father has sent. Hereafter, the Phantom becomes her tutor who teaches her to sing the songs that he composes.

After a stellar performance at the opera house, Christine reacquaints herself with her childhood companion and sweetheart Raulle who recognizes her on stage. She tells him about the "angel of music" and says that she must obey him, but Raulle doesn't believe that the angel is real.

Threatened by her new suitor, the Phantom of the Opera woos Christine with promises of his dark sensual love for her. He takes her to his underground dwelling beneath the opera house and sings to her the songs of the music of the night.

"Touch me, trust me, savor each sensation... Open up your mind; let your fantasies unwind... Let your darker side give in to the power of the

music of the night." She is mesmerized by him and thinks that it is all a fantastic dream.

In his jealous passion for her, the Phantom murders a man during a stage performance in order to instill fear in the opera house staff, coercing them to obey him and make Christine the opera house diva. Christine wakes up to the fact that she is entertaining a mystical murderer.

Raulle also promises his love to Christine but his motives are for her freedom, not her captivity. He sings to her songs of safety and protection.

"No more talk of darkness, my words will warm and calm you. Let me be your freedom and your guide."

Christine must decide between these two suitors who have approached her with promises of love: her mysterious teacher who sang songs to her from the shadows and promises her greatness on stage, or her childhood friend who offers her safety, protection and freedom.

Raulle pursues the mystery of the Phantom of the Opera and finds that the stalker is a real man who lives in the catacombs of the opera house. He discovers the truth behind the masquerade and appeals to the opera house mistress who has been hiding the secret. "Clearly genius has turned to madness," he tells her.

Christine continues to wrestle with her deep emotional ties to her father. She has to re-assess her beliefs and accept the fact that the "angel of music" was a disguise that the Phantom used to captivate her. Under the light of truth, now she can see behind the mask to discern the motives of a liar and a murderer.

In order to stop his tyranny at the opera house, she must unmask him publicly to identify him to the police who are waiting in the wings during her performance. In the final scene, the Phantom once more sings his songs of sweet seduction in order to try to sway her will. Raulle sits and watches them perform together on stage, weeping at the thought that the Phantom may win her with his dark deceptive love.

Fortunately, Christine comes to her senses and resists the Phantom's sensuous appeal. As he holds her close, she resolutely peels off his mask, exposing his ugly disfigurement to the audience and to the police. In a final act of revenge, the Phantom cuts the ropes of the opera house chandelier and sends it crashing down to the stage, setting the opera house on fire. The Phantom escapes with Christine to his underground hideout. But through her resistance to him, the Phantom realizes that he does not have her love after all and is compelled to release her to her true lover, Raulle, whom she lives to marry.

ALL THE WORLD'S A STAGE

Now let me use this story to explain the players on the real stage of this present age. We have the heroine who represents the beautifully fashioned assembly of human beings on earth, created to have meaningful existence through relationship with their Creator. We also have a phantom in the form of a personal devil who hates us with an undying hate and who constantly plans our demise as an act of revenge towards God. The devil stands condemned due to his sin of self-worship and rebellion in Heaven, entertaining in his mind that he would be God. We also have our hero, Jesus, who was sent from Heaven by the Father to endure our pain and suffering on the Cross and to legally pay the penalty for our sins, receiving the punishment of death that we deserved. Because of His resurrection, He stands ready to lead us back into a restored relationship with God the Father. Jesus' motive towards us is pure love and His death on our behalf is solid proof of His commitment to us.

The tragic mistake that people make is refusing to believe that the devil is actually real. All of the trouble, tragedy and interpersonal violence that we see or experience is due to the fallen nature

SEEING BEHIND THE MASK

incited by the devil. He tempts people to act upon sinful desires that bring harm to themselves and to others. Even though the pervasiveness of evil throughout human society bears witness of this fact, we deny his presence with us. Our unbelief in his existence is the devil's biggest trump card that he holds as he carries out his rage against us. Our ignorance permits him to rule and reign from the shadows as a master of deception. Truly his genius has turned to madness, and we are suffering because of it.

Jesus makes Himself available to us as our Savior, Friend, Protector, Provider and Guide via the Holy Spirit during this life in preparation for the next. He has taken His place in Heaven as our Advocate, praying for God's mercy and benevolence on our behalf. This may seem like a very simplistic explanation of the world's woes, but if we continue to delve into the cause of human suffering then we will find the explanation in God's Word to be sufficient.

To go about our daily routines, we would never imagine that a drama of this magnitude is going on in the spirit realm around us. Not until tragedy strikes and another human life is either marred or taken by the cruelty of another person do we see the crossfire between the powers of good and evil, God and Satan. The desperation of people coping with the pain of human turmoil and man's inhumanity to his fellow man gives credence to this supernatural context. Through untold loss, wrong doing and irreconcilable offenses, we lift our tear stained faces and ask, "Why?" Allow me to explain.

AN ANGEL OF LIGHT

Like the opening act of a play, Adam and Eve came to life on day six of creation to encounter the scope of an unhindered relationship with their Creator. They had no secrets hidden from each other. They were open, teachable and innocent as they walked with God in the Garden of Eden. Man and woman were created to be the special object of God's love as they basked in His infinite wisdom, protection and guidance. They knew God and obeyed Him because they were filled with love for Him. He was their Sustainer of Life, the One they worshiped and their reason for living. In effect, He was their world.

This light-hearted co-existence between God and man was God's plan for all of time upon the earth. God Himself would meet their every need in their utter dependence upon Him. **"And out of the ground the Lord God caused to grow every tree that is pleasing to the sight and good for food; the tree of life was also in the midst of the garden, and the tree of knowledge of good and evil." (Genesis 2:9)** Within the boundaries of their relationship, God commanded Adam not to eat from the tree of knowledge because He knew that there was one place in the Garden where evil was lurking. God steered man clear of it with a severe warning that, if he should disobey and eat of it, he would begin to die.

One fateful day, Eve was innocently enjoying the beauty of the Garden. She was distinct from Adam in her refined sensitivity and emotional complexity. She had an eye for vivid colors and detail. The variety of all she saw was a constant source of pleasure and excitement for her.

She looked over at the tree of knowledge in the midst of the Garden and saw something new that caught her attention. She saw a shimmering figure like a serpent beckoning her. Although this was the only tree that the Master had forbidden them to eat from, the strange radiance that she saw made her heart beat with excitement.

"Isn't it beautiful?" she said to herself as she fell captive to her own curiosity. She became fascinated as she focused on the vision. Caught up in its power, she moved towards its light to get a closer look.

Adam looked up from his work and saw her walking trance-like towards the forbidden tree. He followed her to see what she was going to do. Although the manifest presence of the Lord was not with them at the moment, something like an alarm was going off inside his gut.

Eve stood mesmerized beneath the glowing tree as the serpent began to speak to her. **"Indeed, has God said, 'You shall not eat from any tree of the garden?'" (Genesis 3:1)** His voice was smooth and enticing. Her senses were pounding with excitement. She had never felt like this before! She had always enjoyed the pleasure of her delicate senses, but now she was taken over with ecstasy! As she entertained the serpent's suggestions, she bathed in this sensual pleasure, as if entwined by its shimmering coils. Her skin tingled and her heart raced. She felt powerful and alive; she never wanted these feelings to end!

Adam watched her as she started to undulate in a sort of dance. She was so beautiful to him at this moment that he became very aroused. His love for her burned within him. He thought of all the pleasure they had in the Garden. The earth had become their intimate playground.

The serpent saw Adam but he kept speaking to the woman in an even more convincing way.

"You surely shall not die! For God knows that in the day you eat from it your eyes will be opened, and you will be like God, knowing good and evil." (Genesis 3:4-5)

She was intrigued. Could there be something more for her? Was there some pleasure in knowledge that she was missing? Could the serpent be telling her some great secret that God had withheld from them? She immediately felt betrayed, hurt and unloved. Her thoughts were filled with fantasies of knowing even greater things, perhaps even knowing more than God! Now she could have power of her own rather than be so dependent upon Adam. Her mind soon won over her heart as she mechanically reached up, plucked the fruit and quickly ate it.

Adam watched Eve with amazement as he saw her facial features change. She had sort of a distorted crazed look on her face that he had never seen before. She stood speaking to him about love, power and a wisdom that he could have for himself just like she had now. He wondered if what she was telling him could be true. He decided that he had to experience this power for himself. Adam knew what God had said to him, but his desire for Eve and what she was telling him was more important to him than God's strict warning. He rebelled against what God had said as desire overtook him. He took the fruit from her hand and anxiously ate from it.

In a moment, the strange light from the serpent dissipated and the vision ended. They both felt naked and dirty with a filth that they could not wash off. Adam and Eve stepped apart and looked at each other with contempt. Their stark nakedness made them ashamed to be out in the open. Overwhelming fear filled both of them as they fled from the tree in hopes that God would not find out what they had done.

The phantom-like serpent also disappeared from sight. The precedent had been set, the damage was done. Satan now had access to speak to the minds of men and women to tempt them to obey his voice. The sickening twist was that, in their unbelief, they would assume that the voice inside their head was their own.

History has played out this original scene time and time again with different actors, in different cultures, during different epochs. The voice of the phantom, also known as Satan, has been whispering lies to discredit God's Word for centuries. The phantom gives his agents, who are demon spirits, specific assignments to cripple the lives of people down through the ages. This scene comprises the foundational work of the phantom, if we would only dare to believe that it is real.

To prove my point, one day at work I received an e-mail from a co-worker who included me in the correspondence because she knew I was "spiritual." The title of the e-mail was "Friends." It pictured a transparent phantom-like winged figure in shimmering white robes hovering over a pond of water in the woods. The face had shadowy features that were indistinguishable. This picture looked as if the winged angelic creature had been discovered in an Eden-like garden and caught on film as proof of its existence. Through computer imagery, someone had composed his idea of a wood nymph spirit. Under the photograph was a caption that read, "This is a sacred angel." The e-mail gave these mystical directions on what to do with the image: "You must pass this angel on to at least 3 people within the hour of receiving this e-mail. After you do, make a wish. If you have passed it on, your wish will come true and love will come your way shortly. Send this e-mail to all your good friends online to show them you are friends. Remember, no man or woman is a failure who has a friend." Author Unknown. My co-worker's comment to her online friends was, "Isn't this beautiful?"

I groaned after reading this message and gently replied to her that the Bible tells us that Jesus is the only One that we are to have a spiritual relationship with. Wishes don't come true because of "sacred angels" and friends. She was being mis-lead. Because of the spiritual discernment that I possessed, I knew exactly who the "Author Unknown" was. Shrouded in mystery and superstition, the Bible says that Satan disguises himself as an angel of light. **"And no wonder, for even Satan disguises himself as an angel of light." (2 Corinthians 11:14)**

This same angel of light that my friend was fascinated with was similar to the same being that hovered in the Garden of Eden at the dawn of human existence. Human beings were never meant to listen to, much less entertain demonic beings that belong to Satan's kingdom. This was never God's will for us. Demons come to people with the intention to steal, kill and destroy as much as they can get away with. If they can captivate men and women's thoughts with their lies, then they can hold them captive to sin, harden them from a healthy fear of evil and lead them into a fiery hell that is full of torment. This is the true motive behind the phantom who speaks to people from the shadows. He fills people's minds with fantasy notions and unproven myths in an effort to squelch their desire to know the reality of God.

Let's go further to examine more of the motives and activities of the master of deception.

Deception
CHAPTER TWO

*"Sing for me!" the Phantom of the Opera entreated Christine as he car-
ried her off in a dream-like trance in the middle of the night to his mysterious underground realm. He lusted for her and longed to control her.
He thought that she could bring him the glory that he so ardently craved.
She was stunningly beautiful and desirable, and he in stark contrast, was
a miserable disfigured outcast. But now, because she was singing his dark
songs, he could somehow live vicariously through her.*

The devil hates mankind, but he also lusts for our worship of him. He wants us to sing his dark sin-filled
songs, defile ourselves with sensual living and follow
his lurid behavior. This way he can somehow express himself vicariously through us. Satan's motive behind spiritual deception is to
be unwittingly crowned king of this natural realm. People worship
and serve him by doing the dark deeds that he whispers to them.

Adam's rebellion against God was not enough for Satan. He
longs to have a world-wide army of angry, defiant rebels all shaking

their fists in the face of their Creator. The more they defy God and deny His Word, the more they glorify their unseen evil master. Satan's plan is to make people his puppets and slaves, helplessly caught like trapped beasts in the nets of his dark power, yet never recognizing what is truly happening.

The biblical world view encompasses the reality of a cosmic rebellion in Heaven that unleashed the evil supernaturalism that we now face on earth. At one time, the arch-angel Lucifer actually guarded God's throne with worship. **"You were the anointed cherub who covers…" (Ezekiel 28:14)** At some indefinable point, Lucifer took his eyes off of God and looked down at himself to admire his own beauty. He saw himself wearing Heaven's most dazzling jewels to denote his high and powerful position, and reasoned that he was superior to the other ranks of angels. **"Your heart was lifted up because of your beauty and you corrupted your wisdom by reason of your splendor." (Ezekiel 28:17)**

In his heart, Lucifer envisioned himself to be on par with the Most High, counting himself worthy to receive the on-going worship that was directed to God alone. This reasoning was vain, delusional, selfish and incredibly insane. **"Because your heart is lifted up and you have said, "I am a god, I sit in the seat of gods…" (Ezekiel 28:2)** Now, instead of protecting the worship of God, his lust-filled competition became a threat to it.

Lucifer's assault on the sovereignty of God was the cause for an insurrection as he deceived other angels to follow him. God responded by judging and condemning Lucifer along with his stolen army, casting them down to the earth and its lower regions. **"I saw Satan fall like lightening from Heaven." (Luke 10: 18)**

Lucifer now carries the name of Satan which means "The Adversary" to identify him as an enemy of God and man. His main work on earth is to tempt people to follow him in rebellion, leading them away from their rightful relationship with God. Through deceptive means, he leads the whole world astray, living estranged from the knowledge of their loving Creator.

Satan must remain hidden from man's full view, hiding in the shadows to carry out his masquerade. Man's naturalistic world view gears people to believe that there is nothing else beyond the physical realm. Only the biblical world view delineates the spirit realm that is invisible but superior to man. If people see the truth of the biblical world view, they would know the secret revenge tactic that is being leveled against them and would run to God for His protection against evil supernaturalism. **"And the great dragon was thrown down, the serpent of old who is called the devil and Satan, who deceives the whole world; he was thrown down to the earth, and his angels were thrown down with him." (Revelation 12:9)**

Deception is a misleading promise of something that is actually false, bad or flawed but is represented as something right, good or true. The facts are purposely manipulated and not fully disclosed. The truth is hidden and the fallacies cannot be detected. As a result, the recipient is tricked into accepting what is offered rather than making an informed decision based upon knowledge of all the facts.

When speaking of spiritual deception, we point to specialized messages that teach people about spiritual issues but are unfounded, misleading and do not correctly represent God's message to mankind. Ideas about God, death and the afterlife that people have concocted in order to soothe their deepest fears and then present as accurate accounts qualify as false teaching. False teachers are people who influence others by professing the false messages they have either authored or adopted.

The Bible speaks of the nature or make-up of two spiritual kingdoms which are referred to as "darkness" and "light." Spiritual blindness is the term for our lack of insight of biblical reality and ignorance of our true condition before God. **"And even if our gospel is veiled, it is veiled to those who are perishing, in whose case the god of this world has blinded the minds of the unbelieving, that they might not see the light of the gospel of the glory of Christ, who is the image of God." (2 Corinthians 4:3-4)** When Adam sinned, he represented a race of people whose knowledge of God was cut off. Man's mind became clouded by his own self focus which ruined his ability to think clearly. Mankind now operates in a type of "soup" or "fog" of spiritual darkness where spiritual matters are confusing to him. The phantom works to keep the confusion going by launching false teachers to offer people spiritual sounding explanations but with wrong conclusions. He wants to keep people in the dark, groping around on the planet in search of answers, but never coming to know the real truth.

Spiritual blindness works in favor of false teachers and their deception because people don't know any better and they accept their messages readily. This is also a key advantage in the Adversary's plot. If people think they have what they need, they won't question their beliefs.

All people are infected by the fruit of the tree of knowledge of good and evil and we have self-centered human reasoning to show for it. Mimicking Satan, man's sin involved side-stepping God in order to have another wisdom that he thought would make him powerful on his own. The wisdom that man received from Satan was actually a working knowledge on how to rebel and remain autonomous. It may feel powerful, but it has no credence.

With this knowledge, good and evil are combined into one and blended to produce one's own version of morality. Moral man becomes his own self-righteous judge who determines what is right and wrong by his own viewpoint. He holds to his own opinions of "what is true for me." This insight also enables people to use "good" reasons to justify their own wrongdoing. It provides a covering of "good" to hide evil activities behind a mask of cordial behavior. The underlying motive is to do whatever works in order to get by in life. This is the cultural relativism that is on the rise.

We do not have to go very far in the Bible to see how deception was first employed by man. In Genesis 4:4-8, the Lord saw the seeds of anger, jealousy and murder growing in Cain's heart against his brother Abel. God warned Cain that the sin of murder would overtake his will if he allowed it. God spoke to Cain's conscience and offered him a chance to repent, but Cain refused. He decided to satisfy his growing anger by using violence instead.

One fateful day, Abel was out in the field alone with his brother, unsuspecting of his brother's violent hatred towards him. Through some friendly mask, Cain got close enough to his brother to overpower him and kill him. One can only imagine the crushing heartache for those first parents to experience murder and death of their son, a reminder of the consequences of their own rebellion against the voice of God.

This pattern continues to our day. God cannot be blamed for relentless murder and violence that covers the earth as men and women oppress and kill each other. Man's inhumanity towards his fellow man was never God's will for the human community. It all stems from the knowledge of good and evil that veils conscience with self-centered justification. People do not realize that this innate knowledge leads them away from God at every turn. The following are more consequences that still affect us today.

Our thinking is perverted, yet full of pride. In a sense, we are irrational because we prefer to act upon what we think over and above what God has said. Separation from our Creator causes us to draw wrong conclusions about life and to assume that this world is all there is to live for. Our thinking is confused, self-centered and self-absorbed. We see the world through "self" colored glasses, instead of having full awareness to make wise choices for ourselves.

We do not relate well to others. Our love for others is tainted by lust from our self-serving nature. We want relationships with others depending upon what they can do for us. Otherwise, people tend to withdraw into themselves and prefer to be left alone. They do not want to live in community with others because of the give and take that is required to get along and meet the needs of others.

We are unrighteous by nature. Right and wrong are subjective according to our opinions. We are morally outraged by the sins of others but make every excuse for ourselves. Yet, in our self-righteousness, we are not in right standing before God in our sin against Him.

With sin, our dark loves take over and worship shifts off of the Creator and onto created things. We pursue possessions because they somehow define who we are and give us something tangible to put our trust in. Idolatry is placing "things" on a pedestal because they somehow enhance our image.

The consequences of sin make us weak, immature children with shattered self-images and tangled emotions. Fortunately, God is at work to undo the effects of sin through His grace and restoration. **"Repent, therefore, and return, that your sins may be wiped away in order that times of refreshing may come from the presence of the Lord; and that He may send Jesus, the Christ, appointed for you whom**

Heaven must receive until the period of restoration of all things…" (Acts 3:19-21) During this time of God's grace, the Holy Spirit is at work to correct, heal and transform the ravages of sin. He works to bring people back into the presence of God and provides us with a supernatural innocence that was at one time enjoyed by Adam and Eve.

People can have "light" or knowledge of God though a relationship with Jesus Christ. The premiere truth is that we can know God personally and gain the understanding of what He is really like. **"I am the light of the world; he who follows me shall not walk in darkness, but shall have the light of life." (John 8:12)** The kingdom of light is the daily reality of the existence of God and the unfolding revelation of His will. Through Christ-centered living, God corrects our spiritual blindness. In effect, we come out of the "fog" when we walk with Christ. The following are the benefits that can be ours.

We become truly rational. When we choose to believe the biblical world view, we learn God's Word and God's ways. Our thinking becomes clearer because our perspective is corrected. We are focused, fearless and assured of God's love for us.

We learn how to love God and love others in a right way by getting the demands of self out of the way. The importance of knowing people replaces the emphasis on having things. God Himself will show us how to treat people in a loving way and we can learn how to relate well to others.

When we receive the forgiveness of sin through the shed blood of Jesus, we are instantly in right standing before God, yet also participating in an ongoing work of sanctification. This is the righteousness of God. We leave our slavery to sin and come into the freedom of right living.

We direct our adoration and worship onto the Creator accompanied by a right knowledge about Him. Our religion about God is based upon our active relationship with God. Loving Christ becomes a consuming goal as we look for ways to express our gratitude to Him.

The basis for all spiritual deception and the propensity to be deceived is a spirit of rebellion. Rebellion is our stubborn refusal to obey the voice of God and opt to obey the voice of self instead. We greatly resent any other voice directing our life. We rise up with an offended attitude that says, "No one has the right to tell ME what to do!" Rebellion also produces a suspicious, cynical outlook that makes us bitter and angry. We misread everything through the eyes of self-protection because we can't bear to have anyone infringe on our precious life. We miss the grace of God because of such a bleak, negative attitude. **"See to it that no one comes short of the grace of God; that no root of bitterness springing up causes trouble, and by it many be defiled…" (Hebrews 12: 15)**

Because Satan has access to speak to our minds, he and his dark angels bombard people with lies, temptations and suggestions that we assume are our own thoughts. The whisperings of the original lies told to Adam and Eve are re-packaged and repeated over and over. There is really nothing new about Satan's "ancient wisdom" of how to rebel against God. Here is a brief summary of the original misleading lies spoken to Eve:

1) Deny death and the severity of the consequences of death
2) Deny the seriousness of sin
3) Doubt the Word of God, alluding that God doesn't really mean what He says
4) You can be equal with God by having creative god-like power at your command

5) People can activate this power through the portal of the mind via their imagination

False teaching simply compliments the stream of human reasoning that people already have. False teachers are people who digest this stream of knowledge and feel compelled to spread it to others. They get people's attention through flattery, preying on their brokenness. Because they tell people what they want to hear, they are in a position to make a lot of money from their followers. **"There are many rebellious people, mere talkers and deceivers, especially those of the circumcision group. They must be silenced because they are ruining whole households by teaching things they ought not to teach—and that for the sake of dishonest gain." (Titus 1:10)**

The New Testament gives us many warnings about false teachers and false doctrine. The early witnesses of Jesus sought to protect the simple, yet profound message of the forgiveness of sin through Jesus Christ. Jesus Himself warned His hearers not to accept teaching that was not compatible with what He had said. **"See to it that no one misleads you. For many will come in My name, saying, 'I am the Christ,' and will mislead many." (Matthew 24:4-5)**

Probably one of the most extensive teachings on apostasy and the proliferation of deception in the Bible is the book of Second Thessalonians. This letter written by the Apostle Paul stands as an encouragement to persevere in the faith. He warns against the work of lawlessness that will grow until full fruition. Paul gave a time line for the second coming of the Lord Jesus Christ to occur only after a time of widespread apostasy. The word "apostasia" in Greek is a term for a political revolt and it relates to a spiritual rebellion of man against God. This state of apostasy is the evidence of man choosing to follow the cosmic rebellion incited by Satan. There will be widespread dissemination of false teaching that will align people's beliefs in agreement with Satan's human representative—the Anti-Christ.

According to this book of the Bible, God will actually give people over to the power of this delusion because they have refused to accept the truth. **"And for this reason God will send them a deluding influence so that they might believe what is false, in order that they may be judged who did not believe the truth, but took pleasure in wickedness."** **(2 Thessalonians 2: 11-12)** When people refuse to believe the biblical world view and put their Bibles down to accept some other teaching that sounds more appealing, God will respond by keeping them in their spiritual blindness to face the consequences of eternal judgment. This is a very real and frightening occurrence that, unfortunately, is happening in our culture now.

The only hope that people have to escape this deadly consequence is to see behind the mask of the lies that are being propagated. God is always ready to accept our repentance. He will give us the power to live in the truth by equipping us with spiritual discernment.

Discernment

CHAPTER THREE

The word "discern" comes from the Latin words "dis" which means "apart" and "cernere" which means "to separate." By definition, it means to recognize clearly or to differentiate. Discernment does not involve the physical separation of two tangible objects, but the mental ability to separate or distinguish between two entities or concepts even though they may be combined or presented as one. Our minds have the capacity to receive insight and sort out the components that makes up the whole of something. Discernment is also the cognitive recognition and identification of the true nature of something that is perhaps hidden from view.

For the Christian, discernment includes the supernatural quality of having God's perspective, insight and divine wisdom that supersedes our own natural senses and understanding. Spiritual discernment is a special type of "seeing" that God provides through the Holy Spirit. The power of clarity penetrates illusions steeped in darkness to help us mentally exit the fog of confusion. People can have "the mind of Christ" spoken of in 1 Corinthians 2:16 to know what God knows that is beyond their normal scope. **"Now we have received, not the spirit of the world, but the Spirit who is from God, that we might know the things freely given to us by God…" (1 Corinthians 2:12)** God has special insight to impart to people to guide them through life on earth. With discernment, God enables us to identify in biblical terms the spiritual source behind a particular person, idea or activity. This is where the biblical world view comes into play for our benefit.

Many times discernment comes to us not with words but as a "gut instinct" that tells us something isn't right. We may experience an inner alarm going off inside of us that something is very wrong or that danger is ahead. The Holy Spirit enables us to see behind the mask of something that may be disguised. This can happen when someone is speaking to us, perhaps acting very friendly, yet inwardly we know the person has wrong intentions or is lying to us.

This is not only a useful gift, but also a potentially life-saving advantage that helps us avoid harmful pitfalls and detrimental circumstances that may come our way. God gives us winning strategies to aid us in dealing with supernatural evil from Satan. We receive useful insight from God when the devil shows up to do us harm. **"The highway of the upright avoids evil; he who watches his way preserves his life." (Proverbs 16:16-17)** People can guard their lives by acting upon the warning signals that God gives them. God does not want people to be ignorant, naïve or un-equipped to live in a fallen world where people have self-serving motives that are often masked.

Discernment is not "E.S.P." mind power nor is it bitter suspicion that causes us not trust anyone. Instead, it is a God-given gift that we operate in and incorporate into our spiritual life. This is part of the supernatural protection that Jesus asked the Father to give to us. **"My prayer is not that you take them out of the world but that you protect them from the evil one." (John 17:15)** Jesus acknowledged the devil's hate-filled schemes and asked for the Father's constant supervision to monitor what we do not see. Jesus commissioned His disciples to go out into the world to preach the Gospel, but not without wisdom for dealing with dangerous and dishonest people. **"Behold, I send you out as sheep in the midst of wolves; therefore be shrewd as serpents, and innocent as doves." (Matthew 10:16)**

The source of spiritual discernment is the Person of the Holy Spirit. He gives God's people the spiritual light, wisdom and supernatural knowledge that they need from two avenues. We access godly discernment from the Bible and from the Holy Spirit. Jesus said that the reason why people are in error is because they do not know what scripture says and they do not experientially know the power of God. **"Jesus replied, 'Are you not in error because you do not know the scriptures or the power of God.'" (Mark 12:24)** God wants us to know both.

Understanding main themes of the Bible, its history, teachings and overall world view is the most important factor in having spiritual discernment. Studying the Bible is actually like learning a second language. The words are the language of the Spirit and the means by which God uses to speak to us. Through the scriptures, the Holy Spirit is able to bring words, phrases and concepts to mind when He wants to tell us something. As Christians, we have the privilege of receiving God's counsel in every detail of our lives. He sees from above and helps us to know what lies ahead.

Our devotional time reading the Bible is actually time spent with Jesus Himself. When we take the time to meet with Him and learn from His Word, we are giving ourselves to Him. In response to our seeking, He gives us insight to operate wisely in the natural realm and also powerfully in the spiritual realm. **"I will instruct you and teach you the way you should go; I will counsel you with my eye upon you." (Psalm 32:8)** God keeps His watchful eye upon us as He looks to warn us of danger or misrepresentation. Spiritual discernment is being able to follow God's counsel and recognize His cues.

People who refuse to read the Bible for themselves are foolish because they are cutting themselves off from the main communication tool that God uses. Human pride and arrogance makes us want to live by what we think rather than by what God says. We don't value God's insight and guidance because we assume that we know better. Sayings such as "go with the flow," "what goes around comes around," "stuff happens," and "everything happens for a reason" give people unbiblical jargon that does nothing to help them in a realistic way. Instead of lame cultural idioms, God gives us dependable advice through the words of scripture.

The second avenue for spiritual discernment is the Person of the Holy Spirit, who is God the Spirit. I will not go into a discussion on the mystery of The Trinity, but simply explain that God has revealed Himself as three Persons; God the Father, God the Son, who is Jesus, and God the Holy Spirit. It is the Person of the Holy Spirit whom Jesus said He would send as our Helper. **"When the Helper comes, whom I will send to you from the Father, that is the Spirit of truth, who proceeds from the Father, He will bear witness of me." (John 15:26)** Jesus said that the Spirit would guide us into all truth.

When a person comes to a saving faith in Jesus Christ, God sends the Holy Spirit to immediately indwell that new believer and seal him with the presence of God. **"Now He who establishes us with you in Christ and anointed us in God, who also**

**sealed us and gave us the Spirit in our hearts as a pledge."
(2 Corinthians 1:21-22)** The Spirit of God now has access to our
inner being and will bring us the gifts, wisdom, power and discernment that we will need as children of God. The Holy Spirit
constantly brings new insight into spiritual principles that we were
formerly unaware of.

The revelation that the Spirit brings is always compatible with
what scripture says. God's Word will name, explain and put words
to the impressions, visions and illuminations of the Spirit. These
spiritual nuances must be defined so that we will have clarity and
right understanding. For example, the Apostle Paul received his
training via the counsel of the Holy Spirit, but that training was
the illumination of the scriptures to show how they pointed to
Jesus. **"For I want you to know, brothers and sisters, that
the gospel that was proclaimed by me is not of human
origin, nor was I taught it, but I received it through rev-
elations of Jesus Christ." (Galatians 1:11-12)**

There are several terms that the Bible uses to describe the
training that God gives us through the Bible and the Person of
the Holy Spirit. All of these things help to produce discernment
in us. These terms all refer to supernatural insight that is given to
us at various times and for different reasons. They are: wisdom,
knowledge, light, truth, understanding and revelation. All of these
expand our mental capacity to know and understand the ways of
God more fully.

It is a function of the Holy Spirit to allow us to live on the same
spiritual plane as God Himself. The Holy Spirit gives us the inter-
pretations to the teachings in the Bible that would otherwise be
hidden and not make sense to our natural mind. **"But a natural
man does not accept the things of the Spirit of God; for
they are foolishness to him, and he cannot understand**

them for they are spiritually appraised." (1 Corinthians 2:14) This means that God's wisdom is not shared with everyone, but only with those who know God through Jesus Christ and have the indwelling Holy Spirit as their Teacher.

God gives His followers discernment on several levels, depending upon the individual calling and need for more powerful spiritual insight. First, there is a general discernment for all believers for spiritual light into matters. This knowledge operates as an ability to detect the spiritual origin or make-up of something, whether it is from God, from Satan or from man. There is a further distinction that God wants all believers to grow in to separate themselves from the evil ways of the world and from the selfishness of the flesh. **"The mind of sinful man is death, but the mind controlled by the Spirit is life and peace..." (Romans 8:6)** In practical terms, we must develop this type of divine thinking by forsaking our own opinions in preference to God's instruction through Bible reading. We also yield to the directives of the Spirit. Over time, we will become mature in knowing God's ways. **"But solid food is for the mature, for those whose faculties have been trained by practice to distinguish good from evil." (Hebrews 5:14)**

The next level of discernment is the specialization of spiritual gifts given to people by the Holy Spirit. Gifts such as knowledge, prophecy and discernment of spirits all contribute to training believers to function in a particular role in the Body of Christ. **"Now there are varieties of gifts, but the same Spirit... to another prophecy; to another the distinguishing of spirits." (1 Corinthians 12:4, 10)** When operating freely, these gifts are meant to protect the people of God and also protect the presence of God. Individuals in the Body of Christ are given greater insight and authority to help detect the schemes of Satan and of man to stop them from bringing harm through deceptive means. They help to keep intruders out of the Church that would otherwise be detrimental to the unity of the flock. **"…In order that no advantage be taken of us by Satan; for we are not ignorant of his schemes." (2 Corinthians 2:11)**

A powerful example of this gift in action is seen when Peter confronted Ananias and Sapphira in Acts Chapter 5. At the day of Pentecost, there was a mighty outpouring of the Holy Spirit that mobilized the early Church. As a result, Christians were filled with love and compassion for one another, and began to share resources so that no one would do without. Ananias and Sapphira were in the Christian community, but hatched a plan to mimic the godly giving in order to gain acceptance and, perhaps, make more money for themselves. Peter saw behind the mask by operating in the gift of discernment and exposed their plot. **"But Peter said, 'Ananias, why has Satan filled your heart to lie to the Holy Spirit, and to keep back some of the price of the land?…Why is it that you conceived this deed in your heart? You have not lied to men, but to God.'" (Acts 5:3-4)** By confronting this couple, Peter protected the people of God and the presence of God. At that time, people were being healed by the power of God daily. He could not take a chance on shutting down the outpouring of power by offending the Holy Spirit with such deliberate lying.

The gift of discerning of spirits also operates to help people detect truth from error by exposing erroneous doctrine. This keeps the Body of Christ on track by presenting Jesus as The Way, The Truth and The Life. People are constantly exposed to media and the messages of culture that serve to influence their ideas. Members of the Body of Christ will be called by God to specialize in disseminating non-biblical material that interferes with sound doctrine. **"Do not be carried away by all kinds of strange teachings." (Hebrews 13: 9)** Their ministry is to warn others.

Spiritual deception will be a great concern in the days ahead. Many forms of "doctrines of demons" are currently offered to people through teachers who claim to have discovered paths of ancient wisdom. Servants of God can counteract those attempts to deceive people by offering godly counsel to explain the error. The end of the age will involve a "truth war" where teachers will be clamoring for the attention of the masses. Those who are trained with this gift will be able to analyze and expose the lies. **"Have nothing to do with the fruitless deeds of darkness; but rather expose them." (Ephesians 5:11)**

The third level of discernment comes as the gift of exorcism. With this gift, believers are given the power to evict or cast out evil spirits from people and places. This is a highly specialized arena. Although all believers are given the authority, only some operate in this gift on a regular basis. **"And these signs will accompany those who have believed: In my Name they will cast out demons..." (Mark 16: 17-18)** Christians can actually detect demonic activity through information given to them by the Holy Spirit and take action to stop it.

Today, this type of ministry is called "deliverance ministry" or "freedom ministry." Many excellent teachers have paved the way by writing books to help familiarize the Body of Christ with the reality of spiritual warfare. Some of the top names are Derek Prince, Frank and Ida Mae Hammond and Neil Anderson. Those who have been called to this ministry fearlessly handle the eviction of devils with prayer, spoken commands and Bible verses. The implementation of deliverance ministry results in the release of people from demonic oppression and grants the entrance of God's prevailing peace. **"But if I cast out demons by the**

finger of God, then the kingdom of God has come upon you." (Luke 11:20)

God has good reasons for releasing all of these levels of discernment to people. The following is a summary of why we need spiritual discernment:

1) To recognize the moves of God as He reveals Himself and to comprehend His love for us. **"I pray that you may have power to comprehend, with all the saints, what is the breadth and length and height and depth, and to know the love of Christ which surpasses knowledge, so that you may be filled with all the fullness of God." (Ephesians 3:18-19)**

2) To stay in belief, trusting in Jesus and His ability to take care of us. **"The Lord bless you and keep you; The Lord make His face shine on you, and be gracious to you." (Numbers 6: 24-25)**

3) To help us "see" Jesus in order to give us constant hope, strength and encouragement. **"That their hearts may be encouraged, having been knit together in love, and attaining all wealth that comes from the full assurance of understanding, resulting in a true knowledge of God's mystery, that is, Christ Himself." (Colossians 2:2)**

4) To understand God's will for us individually and corporately, and to complete His assignments for us. **"That you may prove what the will of God is, that which is good and acceptable and perfect." (Romans 12:2)**

5) To aid in our sanctification by recognizing evil and turning from it. **"The Lord loves those who hate evil; He guards the lives of the faithful; He rescues them**

from the hand of the wicked. Light dawns for the righteous and joy for the upright in heart." (Psalm 97: 10-11)

6) To help us distinguish truth from error. **"But when He, the Spirit of truth comes, He will guide you into all truth…" (John 16:13)**

7) To guide us and keep us safe in a world full of danger. **"And when you turn to the right or when you turn to the left, your ears shall have a word behind you, saying, 'This is the way, walk in it.'" (Isaiah 30:21)**

8) To keep us free from unnecessary religious regulations. **"Does He then, who provides you with the Spirit who works miracles among you, do it by the works of the Law, or by hearing with faith?" (Galatians 3:5)**

Finally, the question arises, "How do I receive discernment? How do I grow in spiritual insight?" God says, "Just ask and I will give it to you!" **"But if any of you lacks wisdom, let him ask God, who gives to all men generously and without reproach, and it will be given to him." (James 1:5)** It is good for us to admit that our thinking is limited and that we don't know everything there is to know. We would do well to recognize that we need God's help, insight and instruction. We must believe that we are in constant need of His perfect counsel.

God does not show contempt for our lack of understanding when we feel compelled to ask Him to show us things. In fact, the opposite is true. He is greatly pleased to be invited into all of our circumstances. When we exchange our rigid thinking for His insight, then we exhibit true humility. We can have a pure, impartial, peaceful means of solving our problems. We can know the right way to handle difficult matters. **"But the wisdom** from above is first pure, then peaceable, gentle, reasonable, full of mercy and good fruits, unwavering, without hypocrisy." (James 3:17)

For example, the boy Solomon who became Israel's king thrilled God's heart with his response when God told him to ask for what he wanted. Above all things, Solomon asked for godly discernment to govern Israel well and rightly represent God through his leadership. **"So give Thy servant an understanding heart to judge Thy people to discern between good and evil. For who is able to judge this great people of Thine?" (1 Kings 3:9)** God gladly granted the boy's request and King Solomon became famous for his wisdom and sharp discernment in all his judgments. When God sees that He can trust us to handle our affairs with godly wisdom, then He will entrust us with greater responsibilities and ministries in His work on earth.

Let's go on to look at some modern methods of false teaching. Spiritual deception is not always easy to recognize because it can come in stages that are gradual. The Bible describes the serpent who spoke to Eve as the most subtle and crafty of all creatures. We do not digest false teaching all at once, like eating a full course meal. Instead, it may come to us in the form of an appetizer that whets the appetite for more. Spiritual deception may even come to us in the form of some seemingly harmless "Chicken Soup."

Chicken Soup For The Soul
CHAPTER FOUR

hicken Soup for the Soul, a #1 New York Times Bestseller by Jack Canfield and Mark Victor Hansen has been read and enjoyed by millions of people worldwide. Readers have responded to this compilation of inspirational stories, fables and anecdotes so favorably that the authors have produced 39 "varieties" of "Chicken Soup" that target specific audiences. Several of the titles are even marketed to Christians, such as *Chicken Soup for the Christian Soul*, and *Chicken Soup for the Christian Family Soul*. But that does not necessarily make these books "Christian" in nature.

The popularity of this extensive series is mainly due to the reader's ability to identify with tough heartfelt issues such as terminally ill children, the loss of parents and other family struggles. Readers find a glimmer of hope and solace by peering into another person's victory. The power of identification offers comfort and companionship when we, otherwise, might be terribly alone in our pain. The most comforting thought that helps get us through a particular problem is in knowing that we are not alone in our time of need.

"Chicken Soup" offers companionship that speaks to people, even if readers have never met the particular contributor. This relieves the desolation of the situation and soothes the ache in the human soul.

One would never suspect any ulterior motive from the authors besides offering hope to people in the midst of trials and emotional pain. I do not believe that the authors intentionally set people up for spiritual deception or purposely work to mis-lead people and harm their spiritual walk. From their comments about their life goals, I see that both authors genuinely respect human life and happen to have found their niche in bringing some genuine consolation to their readers. I believe that the authors don't realize that they are leading people down a subtle path of deception with "Chicken Soup."

Allow me to describe the format and give some samples of the material, and then we will compare it to the biblical world view to see if the phantom has been at work. Let's see if "Chicken Soup" can be considered as a starting point for spiritual deception. Before we begin, let me first explain that Satan has studied mankind for eons and knows us all too well. He knows what works to yank our emotions, distract us and set us up to accept his doctrines that lead us away from God's will. He also knows that people are most vulnerable when they are in the midst of loss and suffering. When their defenses are down, they don't think clearly and may make rash decisions. Overall they are groping for solutions to come their way. Hurting people are a prime target for the devil to establish a foothold. Perhaps they are angry and blame God for what happened to them, quickly forsaking their faith in Him when things go awry.

In the Bible, the Book of Job shows us a clear picture of the interplay between God, man and Satan. We observe how the devil works to spread his cosmic rebellion to mankind, especially at the worst of times. **"And the Lord said to Satan, 'From where do you come?' Then Satan answered the Lord and said, 'From roaming about on the earth and walking around on it.' And the Lord said to Satan, 'Have you considered My servant Job?'" (Job 1:7- 8)** Job lost his children, his household, his income and finally his health after Satan targeted him with supernatural destruction. Fortunately, Job trusted God through his pain and resisted the temptation to curse God for his misfortunes. This type of activity of Satan is confirmed in 1 Peter 5:8 where it gives this warning: **"Be of sober spirit, be on the alert. Your adversary, the devil, prowls about like a roaring lion, seeking someone to devour."** The scripture continues to advise us to be especially vigilant during times of suffering because that is when we are most vulnerable to satanic attacks. The Adversary's goal is for our utter destruction, but he will do his damage in increments if that is more effective.

Knowing this, let's examine under biblical light what Jack Canfield and Mark Victor Hansen offer to their open-hearted audience through "Chicken Soup." With the introduction, they immediately address the widespread problem of human suffering and step up to the plate to offer a cure. "We know everything we need to end the needless emotional suffering that many people currently experience. High self-esteem and personal effectiveness are available to anyone willing to take the time to pursue them."[4] The authors tell us to read the book slowly in order to digest the principles that they are about to present. They want the reader to absorb and assimilate life lessons from the counsel of many writers. They identify one of our basic human concerns as emotional suf-

---

4   *Chicken Soup for the Soul*, Introduction P. XX1

fering, identify the cure as high self-esteem and personal success, and they advise us to take action to obtain the suggested cure.

The first chapter "On Love" immediately names a huge emotional need, calling love the one "creative force" and celebrates human love as the most powerful motivator on earth. The chapter is filled with stories that herald man's supposed unconditional love towards his fellow humans. They reinforce their findings with real stories but also with made-up fables. "Many Americans are familiar with The Little Prince, a wonderful book by Antoine Saint-Exupery. This is a whimsical and fabulous book and works as a children's story as well as a thought-provoking adult fable."[5] The stories go on to play the emotions like an accordion with writings about puppies and kitties and kids dying of terminal diseases. These anecdotes are real tear jerker's that open the reader up like a can-opener with compelling human tragedies.

But in Chapter Two on "Learning to Love Yourself" we are offered the cure in the form of Eastern mysticism. Jack Canfield sermonizes after an overseas trip to Bangkok, "Underneath each of us is a 'golden Buddha,' a 'golden Christ' or a 'golden essence' which is our real self…our task now is to discover our true essence once again."[6] This platitude now puts the reader on a spiritual path to discover his "true essence" as if that were plausible.

Mark Victor Hansen, who conducts workshops on "prosperity consciousness," tells about a "healing process" that he used with an audience who were instructed to send "life force energy" to a 17 year old girl who was undergoing chemotherapy for cancer. He writes, "I have learned never to underestimate the healing power we all have. It is always there to be used for the highest good.

5   Ibid, P. 48
6   Ibid, P. 96

We just have to remember to use it."[7] This teaching raises some "red-flag" concerns because this is not a biblical teaching for divine healing. We do not have the innate power for healing.

The chapter "On Parenting" echoes the same advice to look within ourselves for power and answers. We read a story about a dad telling his son "all the answers you'll ever need are within you." The theories of unlimited human potential are exemplified in Chapter 5 "Live Your Dream." Readers are instructed to set their own goals in life and then exert the determination to make them happen. We are given an example of a man who wrote down 127 goals of major accomplishments that he wanted to do before he died. He called it "My Life List"[8] and it included exotic activities such as climbing twelve of the world's highest mountains, swim in five of the world's largest lakes, photograph five of the world's greatest waterfalls and eight of the most amazing rivers. These stories and many more completely dovetail the vision that is cast with a quote from Teilhar de Chardin at the beginning of the book, "The day will come when, after harnessing space, the winds, the tides and gravitation, we shall harness for God the energies of love."[9] The human potential movement promotes the vision that man can accomplish whatever he sets his mind to if he just believes in himself enough.

Having read the sequels, *A 2ND Helping of Chicken Soup* and *Chicken Soup for the Soul-Living Your Dreams*, I found the same pattern of teaching that stems from a stream of man-centered wisdom. The authors direct their readers to find their help within themselves or from other people. I feel that it is safe to say that

---

7   *Ibid*, P. 56

8   *Ibid*, P. 254

9   *Chicken Soup for the Soul*, P. 2

the world views that frame the "Chicken Soup" series are humanism and naturalism. Naturalism claims that this physical realm is all that there is. If that is the case, then that premise automatically points to man as the supreme being on the earth. The basic tenant of humanism is that man is the measure of all things and the key player who holds the "center-stage spotlight" upon the planet. The humanistic platform denies the existence of God and replaces Him with man. Its atheistic view says that man is the highest form of life and nothing higher exists. The stream of man-centered wisdom exalts the human mind as supreme. With this belief in place, people can follow reasoning to assume that the universe revolves around us. A spiritualized extension of naturalism bequeaths a persona upon nature as if it were a living organism that responds to the command of man. This idea reinforces the humanistic vision that man has the potential to harness the forces of nature through the power that emits from his mind.

The world view of naturalism can extend out with beliefs that the persona of "Mother Earth" or "Mother Nature" has life lessons to teach us if only we would attune ourselves to its schooling. This standpoint alludes to an "intelligence" of nature and its subtle communication to us. For example, Shirley Maclaine shares "Today's Thought" on her website for June 30, 2011. "Nature is reminding us where her power resides with floods, fires, torrential rains, unseasonable hail, storms, earthquakes and volcanoes. She is telling us that we must find our power and go within. Connect to your higher self and find your inner power…" This message typifies the naturalistic view.

Another assertion of humanism states that man is ultimately responsible for his activities, therefore man must save himself. We find evidences of humanistic thought in the many versions of "Chicken Soup" as the authors offer their cure for human suffering.

It is in "saving" others that people can refer to their intentions as "good." Man relishes the so-called good of his accomplishments through sheer will-power and his heroic coping skills. Holding to these world views, man can claim autonomy to stay in control of his life, even when it spins out of control. So with the aid of "Chicken Soup," people are encouraged in their coping skills and feel better by having some human company to empathize with.

Let's now apply discernment and compare the implied teachings of "Chicken Soup" with the biblical world view and the truth of the Word of God. As mentioned earlier, the main tactic of Satan in the Garden of Eden was to attack and discredit God's character and God's Word to cause man to doubt and then reject the relationship through disbelief. Once that was accomplished, he could replace God's Word with substitute counterfeit spiritual-sounding platitudes that pulls man off track. The "Chicken Soup" series qualifies as false teaching because it truly is a "soup" of spiritual sounding ideas with no clarity of the truth to guide people to the Savior of the world, Jesus Christ.

In the introduction of "Chicken Soup" the authors claim that they possess the knowledge to solve the human dilemma of emotional suffering. They say that cure can be found in raising self-esteem (thinking more highly of oneself) and finding our full human potential. But the Bible clearly identifies the root cause of all man's problems is our separation from our Creator God due to sin. **"But your iniquities have made a separation between you and your God, and your sins have hidden His Face from you." (Isaiah 59: 2)**

The Book of Romans deals with the issue of man's sin extensively. **"All have sinned and fall short of the glory of God." (Romans 3:23)** Sin is the stain of the original rebellion that occurred when Adam and Eve turned away from their trusted relationship with God to become their own self-will agents at the suggestion of Satan. The nature to rebel and to rigidly trust in self is within all of us. Our propensity to insist on self-will is what maintains our separation and alienation from God.

In His mercy, God supplied the answer to our human dilemma not through human potential, but through a Person. We are never told to heroically cope, but to simply come. Jesus said, **"Come to Me, all who are weary and heavy-laden, and I will give you rest. Take My yoke upon you, and learn from Me, for I am gentle and humble in heart and you shall find rest for your souls." (Matthew 11: 28-29)** Jesus not only offers rest and relief from the anxiety of human suffering, but also the power to supernaturally remove the pain. That is something that the "Chicken Soup" stories, no matter how well intended, do not have the power to do. Jesus never promised people a rosy untouched life, but He offered to stand with us and absorb the pain for us. **"In the world you will have tribulation, but take courage; I have overcome the world." (John 16:33)**

"Chicken Soup" was written in devotional form, meaning that a person can read a small portion every day. The authors say to read it slowly and take in what they have to say. The prolific "Chicken Soup" series could easily become a substitute Bible for many. These books offer inspiration from man's success stories but do nothing to correct the reader in any way. It puts no requirements on readers and allows them to live any way that they want. It especially brings no conviction of sin, but in fact celebrates inferred human goodness and kindness.

In contrast, Jesus told us that because He has come to speak to us about our sin, we have no excuse because He has been so clear about it. **"If I had not come and spoken to them, they would not have sin, but now they have no excuse for** their sin." (John 15:22) The Bible is the only book that has the supernatural capability to discern the reader's motives in order to bring conviction. God wants our lives to be transformed from sinful thoughts and ways. The Holy Spirit will show us when our hearts are not right before God as we read the Bible. **"For the Word of God is living and active and sharper than any two-edged sword…and able to judge the thoughts and intentions of the heart." (Hebrews 4:12)**

Just because authors have sold a lot of books does not mean that we should blindly follow their advice. Achievement and fame does not qualify a person to speak to others about their beliefs. The Bible warns that teachers will be judged more strictly because of the influence that they have exerted over others to sway their beliefs. **"Not many of you should become teachers, brothers and sisters, for you know that we who teach will be judged with greater strictness." (James 3:1)**

In fact, the Bible boils down all human achievement very quickly by calling it "worthless" in comparison to the privilege of knowing Christ. **"Yes, everything else is worthless when compared with the priceless gain of knowing Christ Jesus our Lord. I have put aside all else, counting it worth less than nothing, in order that I can have Christ, and become one with Him…" (Philippians 3:8)** The Apostle Paul wrote this from a prison cell but his circumstances did not change the way he felt about having a secure relationship with God through Jesus Christ. Companionship with Christ was more valuable to him than anything he had accomplished during his lifetime or even his great ministry.

This divine exchange of God's love for us and our response of love, worship and commitment directed back to Him is the true picture of biblical spirituality. Our hope in the Son as our Lord and Savior is the anchor of our soul. **"We have this hope, a sure and steadfast anchor of the soul…" (Hebrews 6:19)** As we live a life of faith, trusting in the reality of an eternal God, we have God's communication of His love through the Bible. This is God's provision for our solace. Our true source of strength, guidance and inspiration is through our daily Bible reading and interaction with the living Savior. **"Your words were found, and I ate them, and your words became to me a joy and the delight of my heart; for I am called by your Name." (Jeremiah 15:16)**

The "Chicken Soup" series is a sample of many writings that promote man-centered worldly values and directives. Unfortunately, "Chicken Soup" is merely the appetizer to the full meal that the authors Canfield and Hansen have waiting for people in their other books. "Chicken Soup" whets the appetite for readers whose hearts have been endeared and won. There is a vast amount of spiritual advice just beyond this series that hungry readers can progress to. The spiritual principles that we are going to examine next are the real "meat and potatoes" of spiritual deception and false teaching. Let's go on to look at the principles by which these authors both live and zealously promote.

The Success Principles

CHAPTER FIVE

*B*efore we examine any further writings by Canfield and Hansen, we need to do some research to see where their ideas came from. During the Great Depression in American history, there was a business magnate named Andrew Carnegie who claimed to have found a "magic formula" for acquiring riches. Carnegie challenged and commissioned a man named Napoleon Hill to interview 500 millionaires and find out their secrets for making money to see how they compared to his formula. Hill took the challenge and in 1937 produced his findings in a book titled *Think And Grow Rich*, a classic now used as the basis for many motivational seminars.

The publisher of *"Success Magazine,"* W. Clement Stone was an avid follower of these same business secrets and co-authored a book with Hill called *Success Through A Positive Mental Attitude*. Jack Canfield of "Chicken Soup" fame was employed by Stone soon out of college. He was taken under wing and trained by Stone's principles to shape Canfield's own success model. Let's take a look at how some money-minded people not only made it through the Great Depression but also excelled in business to become multi-millionaires, and hear the advice they hand down to posterity.

Deriving his philosophy from his title, Napoleon Hill begins his first chapter by ascribing power to our thoughts and to our ability to control our thoughts. Because we are able to think and control what we think, he says, "We are the Masters of our Fate, The Captains of our Souls."[10] The main idea behind his success principles lies in the assumption that man can not only control his life but also direct his own circumstances simply by focusing his mind and will on what he wants. He refers to this theory as "success consciousness."[11] It was ideas from this book that christened the now popular "conceive, believe and achieve" formula of the "Positive Thinking" movement.

From that premise, he goes on to teach some metaphysical theories about the human brain becoming "magnetized" by the thoughts that we dwell upon. His assumptions are clearly humanistic in nature because his teachings say that man has the primary role on earth. He refers to the "ether" which is the atmosphere around the planet and gives it a persona of a "universal power that adapts itself to the nature of the thoughts that we hold in our minds."[12] This is the world view of naturalism. So, although he speaks of this "universal power" as an impersonal force, "it" somehow knows and picks up on what we as individuals are thinking. Our thoughts are transmitted through the earth's atmosphere and possess a form of energy that moves at an inconceivably high rate of vibration. One of the first principles that he teaches is that we

10   *Think And Grow Rich*, P. 14

11   *Ibid*, P. 11

12   *Ibid*, P. 14

have the ability to think things into existence. As the force field that holds the universe together cooperates with our thoughts, it supposedly brings to us those things that we want.

He goes on to explain that, because our brains become magnetized by the dominating thoughts that we have, that magnetization will attract all of the things that are in harmony with our order of thoughts. He does not go so far as to teach materialization, which is the sudden appearance of material things, but does talk about a drawing power that is at our command that we must teach ourselves to utilize.

He stays with the theme of using mind power for making money which he calls "money consciousness"[13]and tells us to become obsessed over money in our thoughts. "Money consciousness means that the mind has become so thoroughly saturated with the desire for money that one can see oneself already in possession of it."[14] This type of "seeing" he translates into "faith" and says that when faith is added to the mix, it converts to a spiritual equivalent that is recognized by the "Infinite Intelligence." This is probably a metaphysical label for God without having to believe in the True God, Creator of the Universe.

Hill goes on with more of this teaching, telling his readers to write down how much money they want and to verbalize it. He also advises them to form groups with like-minded people so that the results will somehow multiply.

Napoleon Hill was Jack Canfield's unabashed teacher and mentor who challenged him to also use these "principles" and incorporate them into his business career. Canfield is not embarrassed to tell people that he is making huge sums of money by offering

13   *Think And Grow Rich*, P. 23
14   *Ibid*, P. 24

his own version of these principles in his seminars. Let's see how Canfield insures us material wealth among other things in his book *The Success Principles*.

Canfield begins his writing with the promise that you can create the life you want, the life of your dreams but explains his use of "create" in less metaphysical terms than Hill. He challenges the reader to quit blaming others and take 100% responsibility for their own actions and reactions in life, which is actually sound advice. But his first principle says that you can change yourself, and is rooted in self-reliance and human fortitude. Self determination seems like a winning character trait until you compare it to the character qualities that the Bible mentions. He tells people to give themselves "strokes" with positive self-talk, for example "I feel great; I am in control; I can make things happen."[15]

The next step is to determine and write down your life purpose and then plan all of your life activities around that purpose. From this overall purpose statement, start formulating your goals by deciding what you want and when. After these steps, we are then taught to begin using visualization techniques to create pictures in our mind of what we want in life. We will discuss the spiritual concerns of visualization in a later chapter of this book. Canfield then adds to the mix self-will determination about those goals and says to never ever give up on what you want.

The teachings of Napoleon Hill surface with an explanation of vibrations and "The Law of Attraction" which Canfield calls an "immutable" law of the universe and "critical to accelerating your rate of success."[16] Again, through Canfield, we are assured that the

---

15   *The Success Principles*, P. 16

16   *Ibid*, P. 91

forces of the universe are reading our minds and working on our behalf to generate what we want in life.

Finally, his "Success Principles" turn to the spiritual and metaphysical where he echoes Hill by saying that we need to be in tune with the mastermind, "that is, God, the source, the universal power or whatever term you use for the all-powerful creative life-force."[17] He misrepresents the Bible with a quote from Jesus, who never says that He is a nameless faceless "life force" to tune into, giving us whatever we want. In this chapter he advocates the practice of meditation, which we will also cover in a later chapter and says that you can become more attuned to the voice of your "higher self" for guidance.

At the end of the book is a website and invitation to help him start a movement. A movement is a cultural agreement among masses of people about a particular subject or philosophy. Before we compare these "principles" to biblical doctrine to see how far away they take us from the truth, let's first look at another author who is part of this movement that Canfield espouses.

17   *The Success Principles*, P. 308

The Secret

CHAPTER SIX

anfield's movement has found another voice through *The Secret* by Rhonda Byrne. There has been no small response to this book and DVD seminar. *The Secret* has been promoted by Oprah Winfrey and dozens of other self-actualization seminar promoters.

With a rousing approval by Jack Canfield in the introduction, *The Secret* teaches in detail "The Law of Attraction" magnetism of the brain that was popularized by Napoleon Hill. The difference is that Byrne steps up the personal appeal of this "law" by telling her audience, "YOU are the most powerful magnet in the universe."[18] She ascribes limitless power to the human mind and takes "conceive, believe, achieve" to a new level.

Byrne goes so far as to say that the mind possesses creative power, "the unfathomable power of the human mind to create."[19]

---

18   *The Secret*, P. 7

19   *Ibid*, P. 21

She is not talking about simply taking responsibility like Canfield, but actually crediting creative ability to our mental capacities. We will see in later chapters exactly where this "power" comes from. Nonetheless, she echoes Hill and Canfield by telling how "obedient" "The Law of Attraction" is to us, giving us exactly what we want every time.[20] She plays to our egos by telling us that we deserve all the good things that this life has to offer, and that we should insist upon having what we want. This flattery launches our imaginations into endless possibilities and is the mind candy of this whole teaching.

Her metaphysical teachings dovetail with Hill and Canfield, calling for visualization practices as our way to tap into the "One Universal Mind." Byrne does take the visualization one step further by promising that "when you visualize then you materialize."[21] Her final summarization of *The Secret* is a blatant confession of our innate god-ness, power, wisdom and perfection which are the attributes that were at one time only ascribed to God, the Creator of the Universe.

Let's compare these collective teachings that all have variations of the same message to what the Bible teaches and see if we can detect the phantom at work, filling people with his demonic wisdom that detours them from the Word of God.

Let me first explain the principle of trying to plan out your whole life exactly the way you decide that you want it. This is not biblical faith, which was modeled for us by Abraham. Trusting what God was telling him, Abraham left his home for a country that he knew not. He had to discern God's leading to show him where to go and settle. Trusting God for your direction in life,

---

20   *The Secret,* P. 13

21   *Ibid,* P. 81

deeming Him good and trustworthy, is the essence of a righteous life before Him because without faith, we cannot please God. The Bible tells us that **"the righteous man shall live by faith." (Romans 1:17)** We trust that God has our course all mapped out and that He has an even better plan than we could ever come up with. Any other type of living where we deem ourselves to be the masters of our own destiny is evil in God's sight because He has specific purposes that He wants us to fulfill. God wants to bring man back to the innocent trusting relationship that he once had in the Garden of Eden before the Fall.

We do not know what life holds for us and we do not have the creative power to materialize things and attract them to ourselves. In fact, the Bible clearly states that our lives are not controlled by us at all. **"I know, O Lord, that the way of human beings is not in their control, that mortals as they walk cannot direct their steps." (Jeremiah 10:23)** This is a huge discrepancy between what these authors are teaching and what the Bible says. We are also told in the Bible specifically not to pre-determine our course in business as if we have some control over commerce. We do not know the ups and downs, the successes and failures of business ventures. Again, we must ask God to lead us in our enterprises. **"Come now, you who say 'Today or tomorrow we will go to such and such a town and spend a year there doing business and making money! Yet you do not even know what tomorrow will bring…Instead you ought to say, 'If the Lord wills, we will live and do this or that.'" (James 4:13-15)** James, the author of this book of the Bible calls the type of business planning that is recommended in these success books "boasting." He lists this type of extended willful planning as friendship with the world that positions people to become enemies of God because they give themselves so fully to worldly pursuits.

They have no time or interest in the things of God because they have become so money-minded. In essence, they have declared war on Him and His Word with such adamant assertions of what they say they deserve. "The Law of Attraction" only serves to reinforce our fallen self-centered desire to have everything revolve around us.

The reason why practicing these "Success Principles" makes us enemies of God is because they align us as inadvertent worshipers of Satan. There was a second temptation of man that is described in the Bible. This time it was between Satan and God's own Son. Jesus went alone into the wilderness for forty days without food and was tempted by the devil during that time. The human body of Jesus was weak and near death from starvation, but His resistance to the suggestions of Satan remained strong. Unlike the first Adam, Jesus did not rebel against the Word of God or God's mission for Him. There were several benchmarks that were re-established for mankind during this encounter. Knowing that Jesus was starving, the devil said to Him, **"If you are the Son of God, tell this stone to become bread." (Luke 4:3)** Jesus refused on the basis that He would not use God's power for self-serving purposes. God's power was reserved for doing the will of God, not the will of Satan.

The second temptation was that Satan would give Jesus all the kingdoms and all the wealth of the earth for His own possession and glory, but with one catch. That was on the condition that Jesus would bow down and worship Satan, thus declaring the devil to be god over all the earth. **"And he led Him up and showed Him all the kingdoms of the world in a moment of time. And the devil said to Him, 'I will give You all this domain and its glory; for it has been handed over to me, and I give it to whomever I wish. Therefore if You worship before me,**

it shall be Yours.'" (Luke 4:5-6) The devil was bargaining for Christ's worship and Jesus would not comply. **"Jesus answered and said to him, 'It is written, You shall worship the Lord your God and serve Him only.'" (Luke 4:8)**

The Bible says that the devil tempted Jesus with every temptation, using all of the same false promises and deceptive schemes that he uses on us. Jesus resisted him and the devil left unsuccessful.

The main themes of these three books by Hill, Canfield and Byrne clearly show that the authors have succumbed to the temptations, flattery and false promises of Satan in exchange for their obedience and worship. The promise of financial wealth flowing to us just for the asking is their most prominent subject. In the book *Fast Facts on False Teachings*, author Ron Carlson makes this observation, "Man has a spiritual desire for God which he will either fill with the true God or with false gods. This is universally observable, whether it is the wooden idols of primitive societies or the gods of success, money and material possessions of so-called sophisticated civilizations."[22] So Hill, Canfield and Byrne have set their readers up to pursue false gods of success, money and material possessions in preference to the True God. The emphasis on acquiring created things above having a relationship with God is idolatry.

Needless to say, there are many, many warnings in the Bible about falling in love with money and serving it as your life master. The lure of money is in the false notion that you can have an untouched life. All your problems will be solved and somehow it will give you the happiness that you are looking for. As a result, success has become our "mantra" in America. We say it over and over and become mesmerized by the golden images that it stimulates in our minds to have whatever we want for ourselves. People

---

22   *Fast Facts On False Teachings*, P. 19

become obsessed with obtaining a portion of the world's wealth for themselves.

Yet the Bible warns, **"Keep your lives free from the love of money and be content with what you have..."** (Hebrews 13:5-6) The Book of Proverbs warns us that **"Man's eyes are never satisfied."** (Proverbs 27:20) Selfish greed easily takes us over. Jesus told us that **"a man's life does not consist of his possessions" (Luke 12:15)** The level of greed that Hill, Canfield and Byrne are suggesting will surely rob us of any eternal reward. **"Be sure of this, that no fornicator or impure person, or one who is greedy (that is an idolater) has any inheritance in the kingdom of Christ and of God." (Ephesians 5:5)**

A greedy person would be someone who goes after wealth in this world while forsaking everything else. It is a whole-hearted desire for money, money, money. Napoleon Hill in *Think and Grow Rich* downplays the sinful obsession that he is advocating and lists some "negative emotions" that people should try to avoid. They are fear, jealousy, hatred, revenge, greed, superstition and anger.[23] The Bible says that these attitudes come from our sinful desires and that polite, businesslike behavior does not cover up what is in our heart.

Another false promise is the use of supernatural power for personal discretion. This is the teaching about the mind having magnetic "vibrations" that command the forces of the universe. This is the utmost flattery that we would love to believe! In our gross self-centeredness, people would love to have the sun, the moon and the stars bowing at our command. And that is exactly what these teachers promise! "The earth turns on its orbit for You! The oceans ebb and flow for You!...The sun rises and it sets for

---

23   *Think And Grow Rich*, P. 235

You!" Byrne gleefully summarizes at the finale of *The Secret,*[24]as she celebrates all of nature existing to glorify mankind. But this jubilee of self is woefully false.

As far as the immutable "Law of Attraction" that all of the authors say they depend upon and teach people to activate—there is no such thing. The Bible does not describe any such "law" at the dawn of creation that was put into effect for man's use. If there was such an unchangeable law that allowed man to just call things to come to him, then God would have told the first inhabitants about it and given them instruction on how to rightly operate in it.

Keep in mind that the original selling point of Satan's lies to Adam and Eve was the promise to have personal power to harness the universe through knowledge. By divesting themselves of God, they could become their own "gods" and have god-like creative power flowing through their imaginations. But we do not have, nor did humans ever have this type of power in themselves. The Bible tells us that we only have the power to live and move and have our being.

If we can step down from our personal cloud for just a moment, the Bible never promises any of this. The most wonderful promise that we have is that the Creator of the universe, Jesus Christ, gave up His own life in exchange for us, died for our sins so that we could have a restored relationship with the Father. This is a huge difference from being told that we ARE the center of the universe! Let's get a handle on what is actually real and what is far fetched!

These ecstatic teachings about some innate power that we are just now finding out about are practically verbatim the same lies that the serpent told Eve in the Garden. He had her visualize all that she could have and all that she could be, and then insinuated

---

24   *The Secret*, P. 183

that God was holding out on her. He alluded to another "power" that she could have through a different type of wisdom that would be at her discretion. Not knowing any better, she took the bait. One of the foremost schemes of Satan is to trick us into believing that our minds have god-like power. Believing this mind candy, we become so self-satisfied with the measure of power that we supposedly wield that we never seek God for His power. But with Bible in hand, we know better.

If we fiercely pursue the principles as set forth by Hill, Canfield and Byrne, refusing to recant our determined plans, then all we are doing is successfully setting up what the Bible calls "strongholds" in our mind and will. Strongholds are self-centered mindsets based on lies that we believe and we call non-negotiable. They are ideas that we hold so fast that we refuse to question them. They are set in the cement of our willful pride. Spiritual strongholds are the places where the Adversary finds his best hiding places within us to navigate our life away from God.

The Bible does not flatter us by telling us that our minds have power. In fact, (hold onto your inflated hats!) God says that when we follow our own ideas, our minds are futile. Futile means ineffectual, useless and devoid of power. Our minds are not agents of change because they do not have inherent power. We need to see behind the mask and beware of any teaching that says otherwise. We are being told what we want to hear rather than what we need to hear. **"For even though they knew God, they did not honor Him as God, or give thanks; but they became futile in their speculations and their foolish heart was darkened. Professing to be wise, they became fools...for they exchanged the truth of God for a lie and worshiped and served the creature rather than the Creator, who is blessed forever." (Romans 1: 21, 22, 25)** We think we are so smart, yet if we believe all of this, we are fools and don't even realize it.

We are being told by these authors that through visualization techniques, we can actually materialize matter, and that our minds have creative power. If that were true (and it is not!) then that ability would put us equal with God Himself which is the very essence of the cosmic rebellion of Satan. We have to see how these teachings potentially rob us of the most wonderful relationship with God through Christ. Otherwise, we are declaring war on Him by joining with Satan as one of his followers in rebellion. There are consequences to following *The Success Principles* that these authors do not warn about and are obviously not aware of. God says that if we choose to keep going in the opposite direction, that He won't fight us after awhile and will turn us over to our own self-will choices. **"God gave them over to a depraved mind… being filled with all unrighteousness, wickedness, greed, evil, full of envy, murder, strife, deceit…" (Romans 1:28-32)**

In our spiritual blindness, we will not discern that something is very, very wrong with the way we are living. Like Jack Canfield who glories in all his wealth, travel and worldwide influence, we will not know that we are separated from the Living God and neither will we care. The Bible attempts to get us back on the right track. **"Seek first the kingdom of God and His righteousness, and all these things will be given to you as well." (Matthew 6:33)** We are told to seek God and His right ways first and He will supply our needs. We will find Him when we seek relationship with Him and leave the acquisition of material goods up to Him.

It is only in this place of being in Christ that God will reveal our true purpose for our existence. **"I cry to God the Most High, to God who fulfills His purpose for me." (Psalm**

57:2) This is the place of true fulfillment and human satisfaction. We dare not get side-tracked with lesser goals and miss what God has for us. **"For we are His workmanship, created in Christ Jesus for good works, which God prepared beforehand, that we should walk in them." (Ephesians 2:10)** Rather than make lists and become adamant about what we decide that we want in life, we need to allow our Creator to have His say and show us the wonderful God-sized good works that have been hatched in Heaven. Those are the activities that we involve ourselves with and do by faith. Rather than trying to help ourselves to a big portion of the world's "pie," we need to believe that God has important works to be done that are eternal in nature. We should not miss our opportunity to see what living is really all about!

Let's go on to look at the practices of creative visualization, meditation, and Yoga to see the spiritual paths that other authors suggest that we participate in.

Meditation, Visualization and Yoga

CHAPTER SEVEN

The front label of Lipton "Cup-A-Soup" tells us to "Relax and take a Cup-A Soup break." In the same way, the co-authors of "Chicken Soup" tell us to do the same thing; relax, relax, relax and relieve worldly stress through meditation. Jack Canfield gives his hearty endorsement to a book by Victor N. Davich called *The Best Guide to Meditation,* saying that this practice "helps humankind in the quest for connection with something greater than itself—with the goal of becoming enlightened."[25] The forward was written by Canfield. Again, he helps cast a vision for mankind that is not biblical and that we cannot ignore. Investigation of the practice of meditation will give us the insight on how these self-willed achievers are getting their

---

25   *The Best Guide To Meditation*, Forward

ideas and the power for all that they do. This chapter will expose some of the devil's counterfeits that, again, lure people into thinking and believing that they have personal power because they have supernatural encounters with a spiritual force.

The term "enlightened" or "enlightenment" that Canfield says all mankind needs is a term that is used to describe the achievement of a mystical experience when people become "awakened" or aware of god-consciousness and united with "The One."[26] This is supposedly the ultimate spiritual experience that makes a person joined with God.

This state of enlightenment is not advertised for beginners of meditation, but offered later after people become regular practitioners. For beginners, the promises of reduced stress, deep peace, renewed energy and vigorous health are all promised as a result of daily meditation. In *The Best Guide To Meditation*, Victor N. Davich simplifies the definition as this: "Meditation is the art of opening to each moment with calm awareness."[27] He also entices people with a desire for knowledge with this claim: "Meditation is an inexhaustible, continual source of energy, insight and true wisdom."[28]

Before we go any further, we find a "red flag" concern on the cover page of his book. There is a disclaimer saying that the author and publishers do not accept any legal responsibility for any problems that may arise from the use of the methods and practices described within its contents. How odd! I have been writing books on Christian spiritual practices for 20 years and I have never felt the need to insert such a disclaimer to protect me legally. If the author felt compelled to add this warning, then there must be

---

26   *Harper's Paranormal Encyclopedia*, P. 387

27   *The Best Guide To Meditation*, P. 31

28   *Ibid*, P. 31

some detrimental aspects to meditation that he is not disclosing in his book.

In order to obtain a fully informed perspective on meditation and perhaps understand what the disclaimer is all about, we need to trace this practice back to its origin. Davich says that it is an ages-old practice that has its roots in major world religions. Specifically, those religions are Buddhism and Hinduism. Meditation was first practiced and became one of the teachings of Buddha or "The Enlightened One," who was born 566 B.C. as Siddhartha Guatama. His "awakening" came when he was a youth and an avid practitioner of martial arts. One day as he sat by himself under a fig tree and meditated, the spirit Mara came to him. Mara is the "god of death" and personification of evil, which is the equivalent of the devil.[29] This probably was a powerful demon giving him false knowledge because, after this encounter, Siddhartha told stories of illogical folklore along with "noble truths" that he received during his times of meditation. At one point, the Buddha spent seven days in meditation. During this extended time of meditation, he received many teachings of more "noble truths" along with more fantastic folklore. These were demon-inspired spiritual messages. He then spent 45 years evangelizing throughout northeastern India, teaching the messages he had received.

Buddhism became widespread in the East until the nineteenth century when the Transcendentalists (i.e. Emerson and Thoreau) and The Theosophical Society (those who had become interested in the occult) in the United States began to explore Eastern religious philosophies. The how-to's of Buddhist meditation techniques have since been refined and integrated as acceptable practices for use in the West.

---

29 *Harper's Paranormal Encyclopedia*, P. 73

The origin of Hinduism has a much less defined background, having no single historical founder or a unified belief system.[30] Even so, there are certain practices and beliefs, such as reincarnation and meditation, that are central to the concept of being a Hindu. Hinduism is characterized as polytheistic, meaning a belief in many gods (some sources say as many as 300,000) with teachings on how man should interact with these deities. The main vehicle for this interaction is meditation. "The place of the interaction of the sacred with the human is the place of meditation..."[31]

Meditation not only becomes a point of contact for humans to get in touch with their deities, but Hinduism also teaches that the meditator can, in effect, become one with the deity during the meditative time. Research shows that these contacts can have unexpectedly dangerous results. "Should the divine interact with the human outside ritual contexts, such as an unexpected possession illness, then the unlooked-for meditation might not be welcome and, indeed, could be dangerous."[32] This means that the human contact with spiritual entities could get out of hand with unpleasant, if not dangerous results that are beyond the control of the meditator. Now we can fully understand the disclaimer that the author of "Best Guide" inserts. His instructions to his readers have been "Americanized" and are devoid of the ancient Hindu rituals that offer a more controlled experience.

Let's go to the more positive side of meditation that the author presents with claims to be a panacea to cure society's ills. Davich says that meditation is a way to get in touch with ourselves and also to get in touch with the universe. By doing so, we can become

---

30   *An Introduction to Hinduism*, P. 6

31   *Ibid,* P. 14

32   *Ibid,* P. 15

serene, more efficient and more successful. Davich promises that, by utilizing this practice, we can make our lives richer, happier, calmer and fuller. We can also relieve stress, get in touch with our emotions, reduce chronic pain, and the list goes on.

Throughout the book, Davich uses quotes by religious leaders and excerpts from various religions to back up his findings. Unfortunately, he consistently mis-quotes the Bible, taking its teachings out of context. In one section he actually lists Jesus of Nazareth as one of the teachers who endorsed meditation techniques as Davich presents them.[33] He builds his case for encompassing Christianity through a speech from the Dali Lama who also promotes meditation, "Two principle types of Tibetan meditation, one contemplative and the other focused, can be applied to Christian worship…"[34]

Before the author gives us the "nuts and bolts" of how to meditate, we hit another bump in the road to enlightenment with another disclaimer called "Spiritual First-Aid." He says that he has tooled his book specifically for beginners, but if the practitioner experiences any type of "strong energy serge," inferring that the experience gets out of control, then the person should focus on the growing mass of energy inside his chest and attempt to exhale or breathe it out. "When your body feels empty of the energy, stop and end your meditation."[35] Throughout the book, the author assures us that these practices are not only safe and harmless, but also helpful. He promises that it will be a positive experience, but then deception only presents the benefits and not the detriments.

---

33   *The Best Guide to Meditation*, P. 33

34   *Ibid*, P. 35

35   *Ibid*, P. 37

Let's keep going with our investigation. To begin the meditation process, we are instructed to sit in a quiet comfortable place and begin to focus on our breathing. "Keeping the back straight not only helps you to stay awake, it allows in unimpeded circulation of your 'Ch'i,' the vital life-force energy of the body."[36] The "Ch'i" is the name for the universal life-force known by other names in Eastern religions that supposedly permeates all nature and all things of the universe. The Chinese term is "Qi" and literally means, "breath," "gas," or "ether."[37] This is what Napoleon Hill built his platitudes upon as he described the surrounding atmosphere in metaphysical terms. He was not talking about breathing air through the lungs, but allowing spiritual forces to permeate people.

Davich is telling people to sit straight so that the flow of the Ch'i will not be obstructed. Through concentrated breathing techniques, one syllable words and visualization, people posture themselves for this universal life-force to enter and fill their inner being. "Nevertheless, your breath supplies power for perhaps the most fantastic voyage you will embark on; a veritable journey to your Center and the outer reaches of the universe."[38] Meditators are told to visualize or focus on their gods or qualities of their gods. Davich has successfully taught his readers how to come into contact with the spiritual realm of darkness through covert terms aimed at beginners whose hopes are merely to relieve stress and lighten their daily load.

Dave Hunt, author of *The Cult Explosion*, has done arduous research on exposing the underlying aspects of such practices. He

---

36   *Ibid*, P. 81

37   *Harper's Paranormal Encyclopedia*, P. 627

38   *The Best Guide To Meditation*, P. 47

says, "Through various occultic devices and techniques... yoga and other forms of Eastern mysticism (TM), modern man is seeking to tune into a mysterious force that many scientist suspect is the primary element in the universe. In the process, we are discovering that consciousness may involve 'higher states' where hidden powers of the mind lie awaiting discovery."[39] He goes on to explain that this quest only leads people into a realm that is demonic in nature.

Before we finish with "Best Guide," let's take a look at the man who made meditation techniques not only available, but also acceptable to our previously hailed Christian America. Anyone who was alive during the 1960's in America knows that it was a time of unrest and widespread rebellion by the youth, later dubbed "the counter culture." It was this pocket of society that embraced Eastern mysticism along with sex, drugs and rock and roll as emblems of their cause. As mentioned before, all false teaching stems from a spirit of rebellion or lawlessness. In her rebellious state America had perfectly prepared herself to receive her emissary from India, the Maharishi Mahesh Yogi, the man who re-tooled the practices of Hinduism and sold them on a wide scale to Americans.

As a chosen disciple of the Hindu Monk Guru Dev, Mahesh gave himself wholeheartedly to his teachings. "The whole purpose was just to attune myself with Guru Dev, and that was all I wanted to do,"[40] he is quoted in his biography. After a year and a half of seclusion in a cave, the Maharishi emerged and began to teach his knowledge in India. He believed that America would also be open to his teachings and so he came to the U.S. in 1958. After spending some time in Hawaii and Los Angeles, CA, the Maharishi appeared

---

39 *The Cult Explosion*, P. 9

40 *The Maharishi*, P. 17

for a speech at the Hollywood Actor's Club. In the audience was a woman named Mrs. Helena Olson who was so enthralled by the Maharishi's wisdom that she invited him to come and stay as her house guest. Mrs. Olson and her husband were practicing Christians, but were undiscerning about the background of the meditation practices that Maharishi was preparing to unleash. "Roland Olson sought reassurance that the method of meditation the Maharishi taught them did not conflict with Christianity."[41] Unfortunately his practices did conflict, but they didn't realize it at the time.

This unknowing couple offered to hold meetings in their home for people to come and hear the Maharishi speak. Thanks to their hospitality, they successfully helped to establish the Maharishi's platform and influence in this country, birthing Transcendental Meditation otherwise known as the TM Movement. Who would have thought that a Christian couple would effectively launch the man who made meditation an acceptable practice in America and is sometimes referred to as the "Father of the New Age Movement?" The Maharishi relentlessly carried the vision that had been instilled in him by Guru Dev: "to carry on the work of the Spiritual Regeneration Movement and work to enlighten all men everywhere."[42] This would include providing a simple easy method of meditation so as to infuse this system into everyday life. Notice how this vision of world-wide enlightenment is captured and furthered by Jack Canfield and Victor N. Davich.

Let's complete our investigation of "Best Guide." After teaching us the basic breathing techniques, Davich then adds the use of a "mantra." Again, the novice is not warned that the mantras that

---

41   *The Maharishi*, P. 41

42   *Ibid*, P. 33

come from Hindu practices are actually the names of Hindu deities. The meditator focuses and calls upon the name of that deity. Dave Hunt gives a testimony from a woman who came out as an instructor in the TM Movement. "We were told to tell them that the mantra we gave them was a meaningless sound, the repetition of which would help them relax—whereas it was really the name of a Hindu deity with tremendous occult powers behind it."[43]

Along with the mantra, Davich advocates certain postures including the lotus position and the use of visualization to enhance the meditation experience. Anything to stimulate the Ch'i is assimilated into this practice. He goes on to explain some of the history and examples of meditation in other cultures. We are then taught that some of the enhancements include awareness on the job, at home and in our sexual relationships. Finally, he offers resources for teachers, magazines and retreats that the reader can use to further his meditative skills.

Before we un-mask the truth behind meditation, let's look at two companion practices that Davich says are helpful. These would be creative visualization and Yoga.

VISUALIZATION

"Creative visualization" is a technique using your imagination to create images of something that you want and, supposedly, it will happen just as you imagined it. The underlying premise is that people possess god-like creative power within their minds. Several authors who have written on the topic tell their readers that their thoughts can create their reality. By making a decision about what he wants, the practitioner can willfully conjure up a picture during

---

43 *The Cult Explosion*, P. 11

meditation and then expect to receive what he pictured. The principle is that physical matter is evoked by the human imagination.

This practice is combined with meditation along with verbal affirmations, speaking what one is envisioning. Visualization author Shaki Gawain also teaches "The Law of Attraction" that is presented by Rhonda Byrne. She asserts that our thoughts are energy and that like types of energy are attracted to each other. Creative visualization is a way to control and, in fact, compose those thoughts by picturing exactly what we want to happen. "Thoughts and feelings have their own magnetic energy that attracts energy of similar nature."[44]

Visualization teachers then take us down the occultic path of guided imagery in order to meet our "spirit guide" or "guardian angel." Through meditation and focused breathing, meditators go down into self and begin to experience a flow of energy. "Almost any form of meditation will eventually take you to an experience of your spiritual source, or your higher self." From this place, teachers coach you to meet and greet your "inner guide," "guardian angel," or whatever you want to call it.

One author does address the rather scary side of meeting with spirit guides. "You might be surprised at your guardian angel… If the figure that appears seems aggressive or threatening, you can send it away immediately."[45] This author does not dwell on the unpleasant experiences because he has an extreme interest in guardian angels and meets with his every time he has a problem to solve. But again, we need to be concerned about spiritual encounters that may be life threatening.

---

44   *Creative Visualization*, P. 53

45   *Beginners Guide To Visualization*, P. 154

Before we un-mask creative visualization, we will look at one more practice that the prior authors promote. Then I will give the biblical explanation for all of this. Let's examine the ever popular practice of Yoga, which is taught as a series of stretching exercises and is offered at YMCA's around the country.

YOGA

Regular practitioners of Yoga say that it is more of a "path" than a religion. If that is so, then where does this path lead? Yoga is an ancient practice that was incorporated into both the Buddhist and Hindu religions. The word "Yoga" in Sanskrit means "to harness horses to a chariot."[46] but it can also mean "union." [47] So the question becomes, "Union with what or with whom?"

Although it is mainly used in the West as breathing and stretching exercises, the actual goal is to discipline the body in order to move the mind off of self and become one with the "universal force." "The goal of all of them (different types of Yoga) is to liberate the spirit from matter and join the Absolute."[48]

The author of *The Deeper Dimensions of Yoga* makes a similar observation that Yoga is mainly used for physical exercise in the West. He notes that the true purpose for Yoga is not the discipline of the body, but in fact to make it subject to the mind. "More importantly, the postures are only the 'skin of Yoga'…At the heart of Yoga is the realization of the transcendental reality itself, however it may be conceived."[49] He goes on to explain, "Thus, Yoga is a

---

46   *Harper's Paranormal Encyclopedia*, P. 657

47   *The Cult Explosion*, P. 9

48   *Harper's Paranormal Encyclopedia*, P. 657

49   *The Deeper Dimensions of Yoga*, P. 3

comprehensive way of life in which the ultimate Reality, or Spirit, is given precedence over other concerns."[50]

Sarah Powers, a Yoga instructor and metaphysical teacher explains that, "While doing asana and Prana Yoga (yogic breathing) practice... I was readying myself for meditation."[51]

We usually think of Yoga in terms of stoic poses called "asanas" that we see in fitness magazines. The form of Yoga which uses asanas, called Hatha Yoga, is used for the purification of the body. Ideally, the purification leads to harmony of mental and spiritual progress. Unbeknownst to novices, it is Hatha Yoga that carries the most potential for spiritual danger. "Hatha" means "force" or "forceful" and is named for its belief in the awakening of the "kundalini" force to arise. In Sanskrit, "kundalini" means "snake" or "serpent power" and holds that a serpent is coiled snake-like at the base of the human spine. Part of Hatha Yoga is to awaken or to raise the "kundalini" power. Reports from people who have experienced this power say that it is enormous and beyond description, perhaps even unbearable. The phenomena associated with it could include physical sensations, pain, visions, brilliant lights, super lucidity and transcendence of self. "Kundalini has been described as liquid fire and liquid light."[52]

Although not all types of Yoga seek to tap into this force, this phenomena gives us better insight into the true nature of Yoga practices. On one level, the physical body is strengthened and disciplined through breathing and stances that train people in balance. But this is all preparation for the second level, which is to put off the concerns of the body and cultivate the spiritual dimen-

---

50   *Ibid*, P. 7

51   *Shambahla Sun*, P. 60

52   *Harper's Paranormal Encyclopedia*, P. 319

sions, even to the point of somehow becoming united with the so called divine.[53]

Westerners are quickly breaking into the second dimension of Yoga, leaving the basics of physical training behind them. An article in the local Cleveland, Ohio newspaper, *"The Cleveland Plain Dealer,"* covered a story about a local group who were trained in the discipline of fire walking, which is walking barefoot over an eight foot bed of hot coals. The article stated, "Five Yoga students applied mind over matter, in the form of hot coals, Saturday night. The group spent 90 minutes meditating and preparing before they each chanted their way across what had been a fiery blaze."[54] Again, we see the goal of "mind over matter" to train the mind with the aid of meditation and Eastern mysticism to somehow overpower and prove our supremacy over the elements of nature.

Let's look at all of these practices from a biblical perspective in order to un-mask Satan's counterfeits.

---

53 *The Deeper Dimensions of Yoga*, P. 41

54 *The Cleveland Plain Dealer*, Oct. 19, 2008

Satan's Counterfeits

CHAPTER EIGHT

lthough these various authors and teachers who promote meditation, creative visualization and Yoga essentially say the same thing, that doesn't make their teachings right or true. It simply means that they have derived their information from the same source. According to the biblical world view, that source is the phantom, Satan, who is at work deceiving mankind with his counterfeit spiritual experiences that parallel what God offers.

We must see behind the mask of all these practices and their promised benefits to see Satan at work de-railing sincere seekers of God with mystical experiences and occultic knowledge to connect them with dark spiritual forces. Keep in mind that the devil's goal is to be worshiped as God on earth and yet keep the truth of that worship hidden from people.

Let me first explain in biblical terms the so-called "universal force" or the "ether" of the earth's atmosphere that people are working so diligently to tap into. The Bible describes the earth's atmosphere as "the heavenlies," that is a lower heaven than God's Heaven where He dwells in holy perfection. There are several more key verses that describe the prevailing spiritual atmosphere that now covers the earth in its fallen state. This is also the realm where Satan and his demons dwell. This atmosphere is called "darkness" and refers to a blanket of spiritual confusion and shadows from which Satan has access to speak to the minds of people since his encounter with Eve. **"The people who walk in darkness will see a great light; those who live in a dark land, the light will shine on them."** (Isaiah 9:2) The "light" that scripture refers to is the appearance of the Son of God, Jesus Christ, sent to illuminate all men to the truth of God's love and invitation to come back to Him through repentance.

When people refuse this invitation, they are doing so to pursue their dark loves for things that they want according to their own desires. **"And this is the judgment, that the light is come into the world, and men loved the darkness rather than the light; for their deeds were evil."** (John 3:19) This darkness that encompasses the earth and shields people from rightly seeing God's perspective is the domain of Satan and his fallen angels—the kingdom of darkness.

This realm is referred to as a "kingdom" because Satan is its self-appointed dark lord and king who surrounds himself with a hierarchy of demonic beings that he sends on assignments to wreak havoc with mankind. **"For our struggle is not against enemies of flesh and blood, but against the rulers, against the authorities, against the cosmic powers of this present darkness, against the spiritual forces of evil in the heavenly places."** (Ephesians 6:12) This existing dark spiritual realm is actually the "universal force" or "energy field" or "ether" that these many teachers are telling people to tap into, not knowing that there is a demonic being lurking behind this power. This is the counterfeit kingdom that people are joining themselves to through meditation, visualization, Yoga and other occultic practices. The phantom Satan is standing behind the scenes of darkness as "The Absolute," "The One" and the "Universal Mind," receiving man's worship of him as god.

The vision of "enlightenment" that is portrayed by many teachers is actually the counterfeit experience of people discovering the reality of God and uniting themselves with Him through an encounter with Jesus. This is the term that Jesus describes being "born from above." **"That which is born of the flesh is flesh, and that which is born of the Spirit is spirit. Do not marvel that I said to you 'You must be born again.'" (John 3:6-7)** This is the true awakening when people understand that they can have a personal daily relationship with their Creator.

Unfortunately, "enlightenment" is an initiation into the kingdom of darkness through exposure to demonic energy that can be sensed. People translate their spiritual experience as valid proof of the teachings that they have heard and are being "born from below" with a false promise that they are on the path to god-hood. People ardently defend their beliefs in this dogma because the teachings feed their ego. Dr. Ed Murphy offers an extensive study of spiritual deception in *The Handbook of Spiritual Warfare*. As he carefully unveils the devil's strategy against mankind, he says, "Building on humanity's sinful flesh, energized by this evil world, Satan assaults the human mind with continual lies. People, thus being deceived, in turn become deceivers. They spread Satan's lies on a worldwide scale as they unwittingly assume the nature of their deadly enemy."[55] All of the authors that I have cited thus far have

---

55   *Handbook of Spiritual Warfare*, P. 29

enthusiastically embraced the vision of "enlightenment" because they have personally tapped into Satan's kingdom, believed his lies, and found others who back them up with the same information. In being deceived, they have become deceivers. **"But evil men and imposters will proceed from bad to worse, deceiving and being deceived." (2 Timothy 3:13)**

Their enthusiasm about the scientific findings of meditation are part of the counterfeit that Satan has provided through a method that resembles prayer. Unlike the Bible's teaching on prayer that have people looking up to God and communing with Him, meditation has people going within to try to find their answers, receding deep into self. The Bible tells us that when we set our mind on the flesh, meaning self, and use these practices to go deeper into self, we have set our mind on death, actually seeking to go farther away from God in our separation from Him. **"For the mind set on the flesh is death, but the mind set on the Spirit is life and peace, because the mind set on the flesh is hostile toward God; for it does not subject itself to the law of God, for it is not able to do so." (Romans 8: 6-7)**

People who commit themselves wholeheartedly to these practices develop staunch beliefs and strongholds of rebellion in their minds making it very hard for them to turn back to God. Notice the hostility from this author towards any idea that God may exist outside the parameters of self, "It is not necessary to 'have faith' in any power outside yourself."[56] This is a flat refusal to even consider an outside source that is not contacted through the inner channels of meditation and visualization. By assuring themselves that the path to deity is to go within, they have slammed the door on any consideration of the biblical world view that describes God as

---

56   *Creative Visualization*, P. 6

separate from us. That is why this verse in Romans says that the mind set on self is not able to understand, much less submit to God's law, except to mis-quote and mis-interpret it from a self-centered perspective to somehow back up their false ideas.

In comparing meditation to prayer, the Bible tells us to quiet ourselves before God and direct our thoughts toward Him. We recognize God as our Sovereign Ruler, but more importantly, He is a Person to know rather than a "power" to have. So we pray, meditate and speak to a Person who hears us. Because He loves us, He will respond by giving us the answers and provisions that we truly need. **"Cease striving and know that I am God; I will be exalted among the nations, I will be exalted in the earth." (Psalm 46:10)** Rather than focusing on self, our breathing and a repetitious mantra, we sit quietly and pour out our hearts to our Father in Heaven who loves to commune with us and is interested in every phase of our human life. Prayer is participating in an intimate relationship where we express our feelings, our desires and our troubles to a God who cares deeply and understands. This is much more satisfying than using techniques to lower yourself into a deeper love relationship with "you."

Jesus taught us that the whole purpose for prayer was to invite God to bring power to make things on earth as they are in Heaven. **"Pray, then, in this way: Our Father who art in heaven, hallowed be Thy name. Thy kingdom come. Thy will be done, on earth as it is in heaven." (Matthew 6:9-10)** This type of prayer is much different from the self-centered affirmations of "The Law of Attraction" and creative visualization where people attempt to materialize things because they want everything to come floating their way.

People do not realize the hazard behind the repetition of mantras taught in meditation and Yoga. The practice of meditation is a proven method to open the person up to the entrance of demons. By summoning spiritual forces, they are actually taking in evil spirits that are in the atmosphere into their being. Having gained entrance, these spirits can then invite others stronger than themselves to also indwell the person. In both the Old and New Testaments, the word for "breath" is translated "spirit" or "wind." In Mark 1:26 we see Jesus commanding an unclean spirit to come out of the man in the synagogue. **"Be quiet!" said Jesus sternly. "Come out of him!" The evil spirit shook the man violently and came out of him with a shriek."** The word "spirit" in the Greek is "pneuma" which means "breath," but in the case of this scene with Jesus it refers to an unclean spirit or a demon.

The Bible clearly recognizes the existence of supernatural spirits of an evil nature with the word "daimon." We refer to them as demons. These are the workers of Satan's kingdom who wreck human lives if they are given the opportunity. Our mind, eyes, nose and mouth are all portals through which the demons can enter the inner self. When people submit themselves through their posture and deep breathing exercises, they make themselves available for evil spirits to take notice and enter them. This is the explanation for the "energy" that people may feel as they go through their meditation disciplines because demons are disembodied beings that carry demonic power. This also explains the warnings that are posted in Victor N. Davitch's book. There can be unexpected bad results from opening oneself to the entrance of demons, one of which is eventual total possession by the spirits.

In the Book of Revelation, we see a world wide demonization of the human population as people fill themselves with demonic power from Satan in order to actualize the cosmic rebellion that has been replicated on earth. People will eventually declare war on Jesus in the Battle of Armageddon and, in their god-likeness, think that they have the power to defeat Him. **"And I saw coming out of the mouth of the dragon and out of the mouth of the beast and out of the mouth of the false prophet, three unclean spirits like frogs; for they are spirits of demons, performing signs which go out to the kings of the whole world, to gather them together for the war of the great day of God, the Almighty" (Revelation 16: 13-14)** The Battle of Armageddon is not a war of man against man, but man against God in a final conflict to express his utter contempt for God, His rule and His Word. Satan will rally his troops on earth and fill them with superhuman demonic power in an attempt to finally prove that he is god. In the meantime leading up to this final showdown, he is covertly training people to receive demonic energy and letting them think that it is the result of their own god-like mind powers. The five Yoga practitioners who did the fire walking in the newspaper article had to meditate and chant for over an hour until they were filled with enough demonic power to perform that false miracle of walking on fiery coals unharmed.

The truth of demonization (the indwelling of demons inside humans) becomes more apparent with the teachings about people getting in touch with their "spirit guide," "guardian angel" or "higher self." The Bible strongly warns us not to listen to people who speak from their own imaginations. **"Do not listen to the words of the prophets who are prophesying to you. They are leading you into futility; They speak a vision of their own imagination, not from the mouth of the Lord." (Jeremiah 23:16)** We are not to create pictures in our mind so that we can believe our own thoughts and try to make things happen. Through visualization, the demons can come forth out of darkness through the portal of the eyes. The meditator who meets and greets his spirit guide is actually welcoming the demon who has been assigned to his life and is masquerading as a friend.

Visualization instructor Shaki Gawain coaches her readers to show their guide around their inner sanctuary, their precious inner being that was designed to be indwelt by the Spirit of God. "Greet this being, and ask what his or her name is. Take whatever name comes to you first, and don't worry about it. Now show your guide around your sanctuary and explore it together."[57] Yet, the person who does this has just invited the demon to make itself at home and to stay with the permission of the person's will. That demon's assignment is to take that person captive much like pirating a ship to take it off course.

The Bible is very articulate about the forbidden practice of purposely contacting unclean spirits as a means of guidance. The prophet Ezekiel faults Israel for not keeping the inner sanctuary of God's temple holy for His presence. **"You have appointed foreigners to act for you in keeping my charge in the sanctuary." (Ezekiel 44:7)** This was alluding to the real offense against God's Spirit by willingly inviting "foreigners" or enemy demon spirits to indwell the human sanctuary of the inner being. **"Do you not know that you are a temple of God, and that the Spirit of God dwells in you?" (I Corinthians 3:16)**

God gave the nation of Israel many warnings against participating in the occultic practices of pagan nations. He expected them to consult Him, not spirit guides. **"Now if people say to you, 'Consult the ghosts and familiar spirits that chirp and mutter; should not a people consult their gods... for teaching and instruction?' Surely those who speak like this shall have no dawn...they will thrust into thick**

---

57   *Creative Visualization*, P. 95

darkness." (Isaiah 8:19-22) God considers this contact to be spiritual adultery. The Lord is very jealous for us just as a devoted husband loves his wife.

People put themselves into receiving mode with postures through Yoga and unknowingly make themselves better channels for demonic power to flow through them. This is the truth that lies behind the Ch'i and the "kundalini power" that is waiting for an opening to enter through a person's spine. Again, in the Old Testament, God condemns practices that are very much similar to the asanas that people use to prostrate themselves before other gods. **"And he brought me into the inner court of the house of the Lord... there at the entrance of the temple... were about twenty-five men, with their backs to the temple of the Lord, and their faces towards the east, prostrating themselves to the sun toward the east." (Ezekiel 8:16)** The New Testament also translates the spiritual practice of Yoga in a practical way, not to pose our bodies to present them to evil forces. **"And do not go on presenting the members of your body to sin as instruments of unrighteousness; but present yourselves to God." (Romans 6:13)**

Through the practices of meditation, visualization, and Yoga, the devil is able to simulate the true salvation experience with this false enlightenment or discovery of god-hood accompanied by a false peace, a false assurance and false prayer. To disseminate this false gospel are plenty of false teachers and false evangelists who make lots of money and are being highly rewarded with the amenities of this world mysteriously coming their way. Seeing this under the light of God's Word, truly genius has turned to madness as we witness the overwhelming success of this plot against humanity. We can gauge that success from the opening statement made by Jack Canfield in Victor N. Davich's book on meditation: "More people meditate on the planet than those who don't." [58]

From this statement, we can see that we are in the perilous times forewarned of in 2 Timothy where men will be lovers of self rather than lovers of God and they will not want to hear the truth of what the Bible says because they want to believe the self-centered doctrines that come from their teachers. **"To have their ears tickled, they will accumulate for themselves teachers in accordance to their own desires; and will turn away their ears from the truth and will turn aside to myths." (2 Timothy 4:3-4)**

Let's look at the precaution that the Bible instructs us to take to prevent these supernatural encounters with demon spirits.

---

58   *The Best Guide To Meditation*, Forward

Testing The Spirits
CHAPTER NINE

Those who actively engage in the activities of Satan's counterfeits do so because they do not have a healthy fear of supernatural evil. Demon energized manifestations do not frighten them because they are so fascinated with their experiences. The harmful side effects of indwelling demons are unknown to them because that has been masked by false teaching. They don't realize that if they have rejected Christ as Lord and Savior and have made Satan their dark lord by uniting themselves with him through these practices, they will also join him in his eternal punishment. **"Then he will say to those on His left, 'Depart from Me, accursed ones, into the eternal fire which has been prepared for the devil and his angels...'"** (Matthew 25:41)

Humans were never meant to entertain, much less have ongoing relationships with evil entities. Just as Eve gave Satan an audience by listening to his provocative words, so people today are also having conversations with demons posing as friendly spirits.

But their fascination with voices from "the other side" takes them deeper into realms of darkness by exploring evil.

In her autobiography, *Behaving As If The God In All Life Mattered*, Machaelle Small Wright, founder of the nature preserve Pelelandra in Warrenton, VA, has carried on extensive conversations with "nature spirits" through mental telepathy for many years. She says that that she has no fear of them. "In my seven years of working with nature spirits directly, I've never felt fear or apprehension toward them. I've always felt love, protection and care coming from them to me."[59]

During her times of meditation, she describes shifting into certain realms where she can contact the "garden angels" or "devas" that inhabit her property. They give her insight about gardening and lessons from nature. "I experience nature spirits as swirling spheres of light energy."[60] She now offers seminars to train people to have the same type of perception for similar spiritual contact. Her vision is to somehow "heal the earth" by bringing harmony between man and nature. The "devas" are the means by which that so-called harmony will be established.

Machaelle has become very accomplished in meditation to employ specific "devas" to help her materialize physical objects. She tells about those experiences in her book. Again, we see the goal of mind over matter that people work towards through extensive meditation.

The story that she tells of her life as a youth is absolutely heartbreaking. She was rejected by both parents after their divorce and was left to fend for herself as a young girl, working as a waitress before she was 16. She was frightened, hungry and alone for many

---

59   *Behaving As If The God In All Life Mattered*, P. 115
60   *Ibid*, P. 114

years, wondering how she would every make it. Fortunately, a group of Catholic nuns and priests were sympathetic towards her situation and forced the support issue with her father who had legal custody. She was then able to have some refuge at a Catholic private school and finished high school.

She eventually converted to Catholicism and attended St. Paul's College where she met her husband, Clarence Wright who was a Paulist seminarian there. In 1972 she met a psychic named Peggy Townsend who spoke at the college one Saturday. Peggy took an interest in Machaelle and introduced her to the psychic world of paranormal experiences. This training was the basis for Machaelle's work with the "devas" today.

The reason why I mention these details about the author's life is because her story illustrates the fact that the "Angel of Light," Satan, targets and befriends lonely and broken people by offering them love, light and counterfeit power to offset their feelings of fear and helplessness.

Machaelle learned meditation and met her "spirit guide" who offered itself as her personal teacher, just like the phantom masqueraded as the "angel of music" in the movie. "Without talking to or looking at me, he began transmitting instructions. It was if he flowed his mind directly into mine. He started by giving me basics about meditation, and I knew that this was the 'person' who was going to help me, to be my teacher."[61]

Just like my friend at work who was fascinated with the "wood nymph" computer image, so people are allowing themselves to be drawn into contact and guidance from "spirit guides," "guardian angels," "devas," "apparitions," and other familiar spirits who are demons. Instead of being fascinated, we should be frightened

---

61   *Behaving As If The God In All Life Mattered*, P. 90

when spiritual beings show up at the door of our awareness trying to get into us. For those who have a healthy sense of apprehension about such visitations, the Bible offers a very practical questioning process called "testing the spirits."

This test is used to prompt a confession from either a teacher or a spiritual entity who presents itself to us. Because Satan formulates counterfeit miracles and says that he is "god," we have to have some sort of proving ground for a teacher or spirit that presents itself in the name of God, or even Jesus. We must be able to identify the origin or source of a spiritual entity in a biblical way lest we accept the spirit and be led astray. **"But the Spirit explicitly says that in later times some will fall away from the faith, paying attention to deceitful spirits and doctrines of demons…" (1 Timothy 4:1)** This test is the practical use of godly discernment.

There are two specific identification signals that we can listen for in order to distinguish the spirits. We look for a true enlightened confession that the historical Jesus came in the flesh and that He is the Messiah, the Christ and the One who was truly sent to explain God to mankind. If a person, spirit or teacher cannot or will not say these things about Jesus, then you are dealing with a false teacher or a deceiving spirit.

Let me explain why this is so. People who are so rooted in the beliefs of humanism (man is the center of all things) and naturalism (Mother Nature / Mother Earth) cannot say "Jesus came in the flesh and Jesus is Lord" because it offends and, in fact, nullifies these two belief systems. The historical Jesus, who came in the flesh was born supernaturally via virgin birth, was empowered by the Holy Spirit to lead a sinless life in perfect obedience to God the Father. He died on a cross as propitiation for man's sins, was miraculously raised from the dead and was taken up into Heaven before 500 witnesses. All of these events involved tremendous displays of God's power that must be accepted by faith. This goes against the grain of humanism which does not accept the supernatural power of God that is greater than man's power.

In the mind of natural man, he is the self-centered supreme being that rules his own life and imagines that he possess power that emanates from his mind. This is the spirit of antichrist. By his compliance with the cosmic rebellion, he has inadvertently made Satan his lord and master. A false teacher cannot confess the words "Jesus is Lord" because the antichrist spirit within him won't allow it. Since the biblical world view that I just explained is incompatible with the natural man's world view, no one who has the spirit of antichrist can confess Jesus as Lord because he would be denying what he actually believes at his core level. This again points to the significance of a person's world view.

A false teacher may claim Jesus to be a great teacher, higher master or avatar, but to confess "Jesus is Lord" means that he believes that Jesus is exclusively God and there is no other. It also infers a personal submission to God and to His Word, which rebellion will not stand for.

This same test holds true for any "spirit guide" or "angel" that may appear to us, wanting to befriend us. We must determine if the spirit is from God or from Satan. If it is from God, then it will easily confess "Jesus is Lord" and will have a ministry or a message that will be helpful. But if it is from Satan, then its message will mislead and be harmful. For example, I was a member of a church singles group at one time and one of the women in the group was a 65 year old widow. She and her husband had been faithful Christians, had a happy marriage and fulfilling career raising and training horses. She came to the singles group in need of comfort and company after her husband's passing. She began to tell us that the spirit of her dead husband was visiting her in her bedroom late at night and that she would stay up to talk to "him." I knew that the Bible forbids any kind of contact with spirits of the dead and that this spirit was probably a deceiving spirit coming to mislead that poor grieving widow. When I mentioned this to the leader in charge of the group, he told me to leave her alone and let her visit with her dead husband. I realized that the leader did not have a full biblical world view regarding the existence of seducing spirits. The widow should have been advised to test the spirit, forcing a confession if Jesus was Lord. If the spiritual entity cannot utter that sentence, then our duty as Christians is to send the thing away by saying "Leave me in the Name of Jesus!" It has to go away if we refuse it. **"Submit therefore to God. Resist the devil and he will flee from you." (James 4:7)**

We should not try to seek guidance, friendship or companionship from any so-called spirit guides or spirits of dead relatives or even a guardian angel because these entities will be demons in disguise. If we have any of these types of encounters, simply demand an answer, "Who is Jesus Christ?" and wait to see if you get a biblical response. If not, then immediately command the apparition to go in the Name of Jesus. No dark angel or demon can confess "Jesus is Lord" because it has made Satan its dark lord. The kingdom of darkness is ruled by fear and punishment. That demon would be subject to cruel punishment for making any such confession and they are extremely afraid of Satan himself. Satan and his demons are eternally condemned with no hope of redemption because they were on the holy mountain and saw God in all His glory—and still rebelled. All they are trying to do now is drag people down using their deceptive devices.

Just like I attempted to do at the singles group, we are expected to warn others and expose false teachers and seducing spirits. The Bible gives us instruction on how to correct people in a firm but gentle way. **"And the Lord's bond-servant must not be quarrelsome, but be kind to all, able to teach, patient when wronged, with gentleness correcting those who are in opposition, if perhaps God may grant them repentance leading to the knowledge of the truth, and they may come to their senses and escape from the snare of the devil having been held captive by him to do his will." (2 Timothy 2:24-26)**

How can we stay free from so great a delusion that is spreading so rapidly that its precepts have become normal fare? How can a Christian recognize and keep himself from false doctrine that has permeated our culture? How can we develop discernment in order to see behind the mask when the promotion of these practices is on the rise? Let me explain how we can keep ourselves free from spiritual deception using the following biblical precautions.

Staying Free From False Teaching
CHAPTER TEN

I f by reading this material you have discovered that you have been involved with Satan's counterfeits, you have the opportunity now to stop and go no further. That is the meaning of "repent." God gives us the chance to re-think what we are doing and turn away from these practices. You can renounce your involvement and ask for God's forgiveness and deliverance.

If you truly want to be free from spiritual deception and false teaching, you certainly can be. Our complete freedom was purchased at the Cross. This was where Satan was defeated and disarmed. You can turn to God, tell Him that you are sorry for what you did in ignorance and ask for His forgiveness. He will respond by forgiving you and removing all trace of spiritual intruders from your life. **"If we confess our sins, He is faithful and**

righteous to forgive us our sins and to cleanse us from all unrighteousness." (1 John 1:9)

The devil may try to tell you that you have sinned too much and that God could never forgive you. Don't believe it because that is a lie. The blood of Jesus paid the entire debt of sin for all mankind. Anyone who wants to be forgiven and set free from the power of sin can be delivered.

When the "spirit guides" or "angels" that you have been in touch with start to fight to keep their place, then simply address them by saying, "Get out in the Name of Jesus!" They have to go and they know it! If they give you any problems or try to threaten you, then find a mature Christian or a pastor who is familiar with deliverance ministry and has the gift of discernment to pray for you.

We can understand from the many examples of spiritual deception how important it is for us to choose to have the biblical world view to protect our mind. The naturalistic and humanistic world views open people to become easy prey for Satan's devices. Let's decide to keep ourselves free from the influences of false teaching so that, when we are exposed to such material or practices, we will be able to discern and reject them. We must take a firm stand for the kingdom of light. If we make a foundational conscious decision to accept the biblical world view in its entirety and refuse any message that contradicts what we know is true, then we will be on the right path. Otherwise, we will be susceptible to the lies of the Adversary.

The Bible speaks about a "double-minded man" who is unstable in his decisions perhaps because he is easily influenced by the strong opinions of others or the norms of culture. **"...he is a double-minded man, unstable in all his ways." (James 1:8)** Spiritual instability comes from a lack of commitment to the cause of Christ. It is a half-hearted mentality that holds back from full surrender to God. On a practical level, this person operates by his own changeable opinions and is not able to see God moving in daily life because he is not looking for Him. In other words, the double-minded person sort-of believes but he also wants to live by his own desires. Therefore, faith in God is more of a part-time hobby rather than a gripping lifestyle.

The precaution about this mindset is that we will not detect the snares of evil if we do not fully interpret things from a biblical perspective, which includes believing in a real devil. Instead, we will live in a weak naïve state where we enjoy the trends of culture and don't discern where they lead us. Unbelief or half-belief easily leaves us open to the winds of false doctrine.

Another divergent path that we need to watch out for these days is the ecumenical movement of spiritual mixture. This is the ideology of blending all religions and all faiths, including Christianity, claiming that there are many paths that ultimately lead to the same God. Supposedly, the underlying goal is that everyone on the planet should get along and not be divided by religious preferences. Spiritual mixture commends all religious beliefs as valid and acceptable. This seemingly altruistic ideology is incorrect because it is entrenched in self-righteousness and presumption. This places man in charge of the path he prefers to take rather than accepting the one way that God has provided through Jesus Christ. **"There is a way which seems right to a man, but its end is the way of death." (Proverbs 14:12)**

The biblical answer to this movement is that there is no other way to God except by the atoning blood of Jesus as a sacrifice for our sins. Jesus said, **"I am the way, the truth and the life; no one comes to the Father, but through Me." (John 14:6)** The exclusive claims of Christ to be God may raise the hair on the back of our collective necks with the objection, "What about my right to make up my own mind about God?" That so-called right is non-existent because, as created beings, we do not have the right to name who is God. We must discern our ingrained spirit of rebellion as an important precaution to remain free from false ideals. **"But in your hearts sanctify Christ as Lord." (1 Peter 3:15)** The voice of rebellion incites us to fight to have our own opinion, but this adamant attitude does us more harm than good.

Any other religious path that is based upon many gods, rituals, man's works, or occultic practices will only lead people into false worship. People will end up with a religion about God but will miss having a relationship with God, which is the requirement for entrance into Heaven. Therefore, we must hold firmly in our mind that Jesus, the Son of God, is the only way leading to God. The biblical world view holds that there are no other options besides Christ. This belief helps us refuse to accept the mixed bag that combines the Christian faith with other religious belief systems.

The Bible tells us to **"fix our eyes on Jesus, the author and perfector of our faith…" (Hebrews 12:2)** This is referring to the eyes of our heart as we use our discernment to stay in belief. We will not succumb to the devil's snares if we hold Jesus as our greatest love and desire above all other desires. The lure of the wealth of this world won't have our attention because we choose to stay in love rather than in lust.

The gaze of our heart will also determine our world view, which again is the way we see life. If at the center of our being we insist on believing in Jesus, then we will consider all things in the context of His sovereignty. All of our activities will line up in our efforts to please Him. By focusing on Him, He becomes the inner light and focal point that stabilizes us.

This is the love song that we want to carry in our heart that is so repulsive to the devil and his dark minions. They can't stand the light of truth and the melodies of Heaven as we worship Jesus in our heart. This, then, is the best way to deal with him and stay free from his lies.

Obedience to the Word of God undercuts the propensity to rebel. Again, this requires a conscious choice that follows our love and commitment to the Person of Christ. With the aid of the Holy Spirit, we have the means to do what is right in God's sight, even in a wrong world. Because God has made it simple for us to obey Him, we can discern if we are resisting His voice and then repent of that disobedience. Let us not be tempted to remain autonomous and perhaps open ourselves to the patterns of rebellious teaching. **"But one is tempted by one's own desire, being lured and enticed by it; then, when that desire has conceived, it gives birth to sin, and that sin, when it is fully grown, gives birth to death. Do not be deceived, my beloved." (James 1:14-16)**

Three specific chapters of the Bible will give us an outline for the biblical world view that will help us discern false teaching. These three chapters are Genesis 1 describing deity, Romans 1 describing our dilemma, and John 1 describing our Deliverer. These chapters will give us a basis to refute the positions of naturalism and humanism that is at the core of false teaching. Knowing and believing what the Bible says in these chapters will enable us to recognize the false promises and flattery that are offered by the widespread movement that I have cited.

Genesis 1 is creational history that God gave to His friend Moses. No one was there to witness those amazing first days, but modern creation science does verify the events that are presented. It requires no more faith to believe in God's ability to create the world and all inhabited life than it does to believe in some of the mythological beginnings of such religions as Buddhism or the outlandish odds of chance presented by Darwin's Theory of Evolution.

In Genesis 1 we see the wonder and splendor of a pre-existent God who begins the time clock by the rising and setting of the sun and the moon. **"In the beginning God created the heavens and the earth." (Genesis 1:1)** God does not tell us how He came to be, only that He is and always was. So we accept that fact and see that He can substantiate His claim to be God Almighty by the utter power that He displays to set the universe in place.

In verse 2, we are given a glimpse of the two creative elements present to cause something to be made out of nothing. The Spirit of God combined with the Word of God fashioned and formed the formless void of earth into the perfectly balanced planet made ready to sustain all forms of life. **"Then God said, 'Let there be light' and there was light." (Genesis 1:3)** The Spirit of God and the Word of God continue to be the agents of change bringing forth God's purposes on earth throughout time.

God separated the light from the darkness in verse four and used that distinction as a teaching tool to help people understand good and evil. Day one through five unfurls the stunning creative power and design of Creator God who reveals Himself through the marvelous works of His hand. Then He pronounced everything that He made good. For God to be able to speak, bless or enable increase and pronounce something good means that He is not a nameless, faceless impersonal force or energy that is part of the creation, as naturalism would claim. Instead, He is a Person with intellect, reasoning and emotions. God is clearly in charge and in control of all that He created with a purpose and plan in mind. This was the stage that was set for human life.

On day six, God created His wonderful masterpiece, the human race, made in His likeness with mind, will and emotions to gave us the faculties to have a person-to-Person relationship with our Creator God. This ability sets us far above any animal, bird or fish that exist by mere instinct. Man was given reasoning, intellect and emotions, but most importantly, a free will to make choices. **"Then God said, 'Let us make man in Our image, according to Our likeness…'" (Genesis 1:26)** We were created separate from God but bearing the stamp of the image of God. There is absolutely no mention in Genesis of man possessing god-like powers in his mind to create whatever he wants. Man was never given the mandate to harness the elements and lay claim to the universe. There is no "Law of Attraction" mentioned even though Jack Canfield and Rhonda Byrne claim it is immutable. That teaching is totally absent from the biblical world view that is presented in Genesis. We have to be persuaded that those fantastic claims about the powers of man are part of the deception in Genesis 3.

The main idea that comes from the creation story is the account of God as Creator and Sustainer of all life who enjoys and blesses His creative efforts and sets the stage with a purpose to glorify Himself through all He has made. His crowning glory is seen in mankind and the intimate intertwining relationship that God has in mind for human society. He is not a God who stands aloof, uncaring or unavailable as atheistic dissenters would comment and complain about.

The reason why man may sense silence from Heaven is because he willingly ended the intimate relationship with his Creator in order to take up relationship with the Satan. Like an invisible phantom, the devil deadens the spiritual life of man and takes him captive to do his dark will. Man switched masters by choosing to disobey God and listen to Satan instead.

The chapter of Romans 1 explains our dilemma. People are now under the influence of sin, refusing the obvious witness of God in nature to pursue worship of the creation instead. **"For since the creation of the world His invisible attributes, His eternal power and divine nature have been clearly seen, being understood through what has been made so that they are without excuse." (Romans 1:20)** The right conclusion that God is looking for is that man would behold the wonder and intricacy of creation and realize that there is a God who is transcendent of man. Men should respond with intrigue and want to know Him as their personal God.

Instead, man shuns God for who He obviously is and comes up with other explanations that stem from his own imagination. Man creates his own order of no-gods and then fashions images that represent them, worshiping the creation itself. This is the falsehood behind naturalism that gives a persona to the earth and then reasons the natural laws and flow of the elements as part of a "universal mind." **"For they exchanged the truth of God for a lie, and worshiped and served the creature rather than the Creator, who is blessed forever. Amen." (Romans 1:25)** By setting his heart upon self-exaltation, man turned away from relationship with God in order to serve himself with the amenities of the planet. **"But they became futile in their speculations, and their foolish heart was darkened." (Romans 1:21)** Man now uses his free will to opt to worship himself.

Self-worship is the same crime that saw Satan evicted from Heaven and condemned forever. The nature of man has been infected by self-centered reasoning that stems from the cosmic rebellion. Man's adherence to rebellion makes people feel guilty and afraid of God. God's anger burns against rebellion, even though God loves people who are created in His image. **"For the wrath** of God is revealed from heaven against all ungodliness and unrighteousness of men, who suppress the truth in unrighteousness…" (Romans 1:18)

So how can man's dilemma be solved? Man-made religion cannot bridge the gap that human sin caused. Good works, rituals and efforts to enlighten one's self are imperfect and inadequate to atone for sin. The answer for man's dilemma must come from the mercy of God Himself. We understand God's solution in John 1. **"In the beginning was the Word, and the Word was with God, and the Word was God."(John 1:1)** The author of this book is not trying to be mystical, but methodical in his explanation of what he and others had eye-witnessed. He refers back to the origin of time, the beginning of creation and, with this opening statement, says that the "Logos" or "Word" in Greek was pre-existent with God and in fact was God. John 1:3 explains the Word of God as the creative entity that facilitated all things to come into existence. One Bible commentary says this: "The term 'logos' was used among the stoics in describing the principle of divine reason (logos spermatikos) which caused the natural creation to grow."[62] From this opening platform, the writer John establishes the true source of all life and all that exists as Jesus Christ, Who is The Word. He is Creator and Sustainer of all life, the image of the Living God. **"All things came into being by Him, and apart from Him nothing came into being that has come into being." (John 1:3)**

This statement strikes down the claims of naturalism that says the earth itself has a loving duty to sustain its creatures and, even as an inanimate object, can carry on a relationship of sorts with humans and animals. Once again, there is no mention of this

---

62   *New Bible Commentary*, P. 930

naturalistic doctrine that is really more fantastic to believe that a historical Jesus who holds all things together by the power of His Word. **"And He is the radiance of His glory and the exact representation of His nature and upholds all things by the word of his power..." (Hebrews 1:3)** "Logos" would also explain to man's inquisitive mind the real explanation behind the wonder of the seasons, reproduction, growing plants and the whole ecology of the earth. We now have a Name and a face to accredit this marvelous power that exists in nature instead of an impersonal force. That power is actually a Person who donned human skin in order to come and explain God to us.

The next two verses of John 1 define true enlightenment as the awakening and realization in man's mind that Jesus is God Almighty. This understanding also includes conviction within conscience, showing us that our thinking thus far has been wrong and offensive to God. **"In Him was life, and the life was the light of men. And the light shines in the darkness...There was the true light which, coming into the world, enlightens every man." (John 1:4,5,9)** The true enlightenment involves seeing that we are not the powerful, all-knowing god-like creatures that we pretend to be. Human pride is exposed under the light that Jesus brings. Instead, we understand that Jesus has come to communicate to us His role and rightful rule as our Creator. With God's enlightenment, our world view of self as god is proven to be a sham. The only rational response to the light of Jesus is to acquiesce to the true biblical world view that deems Jesus worthy to sit on the throne as Supreme Ruler of Heaven and earth.

Once we "see" Him, then we can be saved by and through Him. Man cannot save himself. How would it be possible for mortal man to cleanse himself inwardly of the stain and reasoning of rebellion? No rules, purification, rituals or complex doctrine can remove the love of sin that lies imbedded within us. We come forth into the world automatically tainted by the cosmic rebellion and each one of us chooses to explore our innate knowledge of good and evil. This is the element within us that we need to be delivered from and cannot do for ourselves.

The Risen Christ is able to come into our lives, cleanse the stain of sin and self-will and, as Creator God, will re-create us anew. God's mercy towards us is extended to the uttermost by the miracle of re-birth, a new start with Him and a new way to live in restored fellowship with Him. **"But as many as received Him, to them He gave the right to become children of God, even to those who believe in His Name…" (John 1:12)** Through our enlightenment, we are spiritually activated by Christ's power and immediately transferred out of the domain of Satan's kingdom into the domain of God's light.

From this place of right understanding, we can receive God's wisdom and continued revelation through Jesus as He tells us about God for the rest of our life. **"No man has seen God at any time; the only begotten God, who is in the bosom of the Father, He has explained Him." (John 1:18)** Jesus is the only One who has the authorization to explain God to mankind because He has been with the Father and knows Him. This explanation of God is much more than a classroom tutorial. It is God using the faculties of the soul—the mind, will and emotions—to be thrilled with God by seeing glimpses of His stellar beauty and majesty. **"…we beheld His glory." (John 1:14)** With God's enlightenment, we can begin to perceive the glory, radiance and splendor of Him who governs the universe with love and power. Our focus shifts off of the so-called glory of self and we become enamored by the greater glory of Christ. With discernment, we can come into true worship of the Creator and be delivered from our

Romans 1 dilemma of worshiping the creation. **"Although you have not seen Him, you love him; and even though you do not see him now, you believe in him and rejoice with an indescribable and glorious joy, for you are receiving the outcome of your faith, the salvation of your souls."** **(1 Peter 1:8)**

To offer the biblical world view also involves engaging the human will in a decision. Just as God allowed Adam and Eve to freely choose, so He offers that ultimate decision to every person alive. The key is that we must make an informed decision rather than having the facts clouded and dimmed by deception. John 10:10 completes the spiritual picture for us by exposing the motives of the phantom in his attempt to pull the proverbial wool over the sheep's eyes to keep them from seeing Jesus. **"The thief comes only to steal, and kill, and destroy; I came that they might have life, and might have it abundantly."** **(John 10:10)** With this statement, Jesus rips the mask off of the phantom, exposing him as the liar, thief and murderer that he really is. Satan has no good for people, he doesn't care about us much less love us, and only has our demise in mind no matter how many promises he makes.

In contrast, Jesus promises us life abundant, which signifies that we can flourish in all ways in our new life with Him. The word "life" is the Greek word "zoe" which means "flow like a river." Jesus is saying that, through Him, we can tap into a different flow of energy and power that has its source in the very life of our Creator God. We can be energized to know Him and to love Him. The Word, who is Jesus, will then teach us how to live in that flow so that we will have God's power and insight for life. Once we have the whole story, we can make an informed decision about what is really good and who has our best interest at heart. This is the place of knowledge, but it is also the place of commitment. As a committed follower of Jesus, we can refuse any and all false promises that may come our way through our relativistic culture. **"And this is my prayer: that your love may abound more and more in knowledge and insight, so that you may be able to discern what is best...to the glory and praise of God." (Philippians 1:9-11)**

The Final Scene

CHAPTER ELEVEN

In the final scene of "The Phantom of the Opera" we see a nurse care-fully pushing Raulle in a wheelchair to the graveside of the deceased Christine. Her tombstone reads, "Beloved wife and mother." They lived their lives together and the time went by very quickly. Now she is gone. Beside her grave we see a signature red rose that we know has been recently left behind by the Phantom. But reality is, no matter how much he still burns for her, he can never have her. He can't stalk her anymore because she is completely beyond his grasp. In a sense, she has escaped her peril because her life has been sealed by death.

In conclusion, I want to come full circle and bring up the one point that all this false teaching and frenzied fortune hunting does not address. All of these teachings, principles and so-called secrets do not present a coherent reasonable explanation of death. There is so much emphasis on getting what we want for ourselves now that the topic of what happens when we die is put off and ignored as if it will never come.

If we excitedly take our cues from our worldly "success" teachers and live as if this world and all its goodies are all there is, then in a sense the earth is flat and we just fall over the edge when we sail to death's door. The earth is flat if we live to satiate our senses with the amenities of our culture and hope to be happy when we get enough. If what we see is all we get, then life would be void of purpose, a life chasing after more stuff.

Some people commit suicide with a "this world only" perspective because they draw the conclusion, "If this is all there is then what is the point of living?" They find out how empty and often lonely this lifestyle is. If there is nothing to give meaning to life then why bother? It is too much work, effort and pain to exist if we don't have a good reason for being here.

Even the Apostle Paul tells us in the Bible that if there is nothing beyond this material world, then our faith in Christ is useless. If this is all there is, then we might as well eat, drink and be merry, for tomorrow we die! **"But if there is no resurrection of the dead, not even Christ has been raised; and if Christ has not been raised, then our preaching is vain, your faith also is vain." (1 Corinthians 15:13-14)** If there is nothing more to be had, nothing more glorious and grand than this earth, and if having the world's wealth, exotic vacations and sumptuous foods are the greatest quest one can have, then all of Jack Canfield's, Napoleon Hill's and Rhonda Byrne's teachings make perfect sense. They will give you the direction you need in order to have it all. Follow them to the letter because they have named the true priorities in life. Go ahead and live your dream that you imagined for yourself.

But if their premise is wrong and this earth is not the most precious treasure to be obtained, then you are taking a huge gamble on missing something that is extraordinary and far superior than anything dreamed of. In fact, the Bible describes something that makes the goods of this world pale in comparison. If what the Bible teaches is true, then the whole paradigm shifts to an eternal perspective and everything is measured from there.

The promise of eternity is the missing element that forms the backdrop of the stage by which all man's activities are defined and measured. Man's perspective alone is not enough to fill our God-given capacity. Eternity is forever and, therefore, it is permanent. Now our choice becomes, do we pursue the temporary realm and neglect the permanent realm? Or do we open ourselves to see with godly discernment the wealth that God avails to us in the eternal realm? Jesus put it to us this way: **"For what will a man be profited, if he gains the whole world, and forfeits his soul?" (Matthew 16:26)**

The parable of The Prodigal Son typifies the lure of the world's riches that puts people on the wide path that leads away from God. The story that Jesus told involved a self-deluded young man who created a fantasy existence for himself in his mind, much like the teachings of Hill, Canfield and Byrne. The desire to live out his dream became so great that he rudely confronted his father and demanded his inheritance from him. The father complied and stood back to watch as the young man wandered off to a distant country. Jesus would not have told this famous parable if it wasn't the universal story of human nature. Deluded by grandiose fantasies, we rebel against our Heavenly Father in hot pursuit of a dream life that we imagine for ourselves.

We all know the ending of the parable. The dream vaporizes and proves to be a hoax as the Prodigal Son awakens to the fact that he has nothing. The problem was that he had practiced the dream of having the world's wealth at his fingertips so many times in his mind that it had become the reality in which he lived.

At some point, the bubble burst and he woke up to what was really true—the fact that his father loved him and had the capacity to forgive and restore him. The Bible says that he came to his senses. Upon returning to his father, he confesses his sin against Heaven and admits his rebellion against his father's authority. We can do the same thing and the path to God's eternity will be opened for us.

The "narrow road" of human dignity begins with choosing to live for God no matter what influences in society tell us otherwise. True enlightenment is when we wake up from our hot pursuit of what is temporary and see that there is something beyond this world that is more valuable and is permanent. When we return to our Heavenly Father through Christ, in an instant He moves us from dying in darkness to living in the light. We learn that we have citizenship in Heaven as sons and daughters of God and we start to act like it. Even if we have attained a sizeable level of the world's wealth, we need to wake up and realize that these things are empty without having a Heavenly Father who loves us.

So the Bible puts our living in perspective, saying that we have an opportunity now to live to please God who we believe in. He has spoken of His reality through creation, through the Bible and through the historical Jesus. The only reasonable and enlightened way to live is to stop focusing on self and turn to focus on God. **"And so since everything around us is going to melt away, what holy godly lives we should be living! You should look forward to that day and hurry it along— the day when God will set the heavens on fire and the heavenly bodies will melt and disappear in flames. But we are looking forward to God's promise of a new heavens and a new earth afterwards, where there will be only goodness." (2 Peter 3:11-13)**

In light of eternity, we are to live with our mind set on things that will last, not the temporary things of this world. We are to set our minds on things above and live by the heavenly ideals that are described in the Bible. **"If you have been raised up with Christ, keep seeking the things above, where Christ is seated at the right hand of God. Set your mind on the things above, not on the things that are on earth." (Colossians 3:1-2)** The power and majesty of the eternal realm overshadows any earthly glory that we have become enamored with.

Running back to the Father, returning to our Maker and coming under His loving rule through Christ, God will re-establish us with a supernatural innocence that was once enjoyed in the Garden of Eden. As we renounce our selfishness, greed and rebellion, Christ will cleanse us from our sins and we will discern the majesty of our Heavenly King. This is the promise that Jesus taught, **"Blessed are the pure in heart for they shall see God." (Matthew 5:8)** The greatest use of discernment is the ability to spiritually distinguish and comprehend God now. This begins with the entrance of the Holy Spirit into our lives through the second birth. **"No one can see the kingdom unless he is born-again." (John 3:3)**

We "see" God when we come into His presence with praise and worship. This glimpse of Him gives us the sustaining hope to live for the permanent eternal realm where He is. **"I saw the Lord always before me, for he is at my right hand so that I will not be shaken..." (Acts 2:25)** Seeing God through worship impacts us and changes us. His revelation imprints upon us glimpses of eternity. We become aware of the weight of eternity and begin to see the glory of it. Our value system changes as God reveals to us the things that are truly valuable. **"Open my eyes,** so that I may behold wondrous things out of your law." (Psalm 119:34)

God is very specific about who He is and describes Himself to us in the Bible. Jesus was sent to mankind as the express image of the invisible God. If we see Him, we have "seen" God. He is not a nameless, faceless force nor a "higher power" or a "universal mind." He is a Person for us to call upon, not an energy field to tap into. No matter what myths, fables or religions man makes up to follow, God has provided one way to a restored relationship and that is through belief in His Son. **"And there is salvation in no one else; for there is no other name under heaven that has been given among men, by which we must be saved."** (Acts 4:12)

Another important doctrine of the Bible is the promise of Christ's return to earth. This is called "The Second Coming." No one knows the exact hour, but the spiritually discerning will be able to see the signs that are described in the Bible and will know that the time is very close. All the more reason for us to stay heavenly minded rather than earthbound. **"But our homeland is in Heaven, where our Savior the Lord Jesus Christ is; and we look forward to his return from there."** (Philippians 3: 20)

At some future point in time, Jesus will gather those who believed in Him and create a new heavens and a new earth where He will dwell with men. He will destroy this earth and heavens by fire, and will start over without the presence of sin. **"But the day will come like a thief, in which the heavens will pass away with a roar and the elements will be destroyed with intense heat, and the earth and its works will be burned up. Since all these things are to be destroyed in this way,**

what sort of people ought you to be in holy conduct and godliness…" (2 Peter 3:10-11)

The new heavens and the new earth will not be centered upon man like this one is. People will not live self-centered lives anymore because self-worship will be exposed as a lie. We will have complete recollection of the pain and suffering that human sin caused upon the old earth and we will not be fooled into thinking that we are "gods" ever again. The new heaven and the new earth will be Christ-centered, meaning that Jesus will be the focal point for all activity. Worshiping God will no longer seem like a chore for us because we will be so mesmerized by His majesty. It will be a pleasure for us to express our grateful thanks to Him who saved us. We will live in love and we will thrive on love because the Bible says, **"God is Love." (1 John 4:16)** We will no longer feel the need to find security in material things. We will be totally fulfilled with no more needs to drive us.

Man will exit center stage and will become the beaming audience, watching God on display. **"For just as the new heavens and the new earth which I will make will endure before Me,'" declares the Lord, 'So your offspring and your name will endure… All mankind will come to bow down before Me,' says the Lord." (Isaiah 66:22-23)** Mankind will no longer be looking through a murky fog of confusion, but will see God and give Him the worship that He is due. The life of faith is to live with Jesus as the center of your life now, worshiping Him in preparation for the permanent eternal realm. **"Therefore, since we are receiving a kingdom which cannot be shaken, let us show gratitude, by which we may offer to God an acceptable service with reverence and awe; for our God is a consuming fire." (Hebrews 12: 28-29)**

The wonderful news is that, ultimately, God wins this raging spiritual war and Satan loses. Satan's single most fear is that man will wake up and realize that there is a God in Heaven who is not an impersonal force, who does care about people and who has the power to deliver them from his dark grasp. That discovery will put an end to his con game. Through godly discernment, people can see behind the mask and realize that Satan is the one who has been creating all the havoc on earth—not God! The true villain will be exposed and his mask removed. The inhabitants of the earth will someday see Satan as he is, a created being. Instead of proclaiming him as god, people will be shocked and exclaim, "You are as weak and powerless as we are!" **"Finally, be strong in the Lord, and in the strength of His might. Put on the full armor of God, that you may be able to stand firm against the schemes of the devil." (Ephesians 6: 10-11)**

God will deal the final blow to Satan and his demons who participated in the cosmic rebellion while they were here on earth. **"And the devil who deceived them was thrown into the lake of fire and brimstone where the beast and false prophet are also; and they will be tormented day and night forever and ever." (Revelation 20:10)** The devil knows his fate and knows the Word of God better than any of us. He knows that his time is short and he is not going down without a fight. He will take as many of God's precious people along with him, those who are undiscerning and refuse to believe in the biblical world view. **"And if anyone's name was not found written in the book of life, he was thrown into the lake of fire." (Revelation 20:15)**

Before this happens, God promises that there will be a final judgment of all souls. All of mankind will be scrutinized under the full light of God's Word. All the masks will come off, the play-acting and pretending will end and the lying will completely stop. Our dance with deception will finally be over. God has a supernatural light that is seven times brighter than the sun. **"And the light of the moon will be as the light of the sun, and the light of the sun will be seven times brighter, like the light of seven days." (Isaiah 30:26)** It will be under this light that every heart and every conscience will be laid bare with no place to hide and no excuses to make. The Word of God guarantees full disclosure of every event in every life, every word spoken, every thought that was in our mind and all of our actions that we made according to what we believed. All unscrupulous motives will be seen; all lies will be detected and unraveled because truth will have the final say. **"And there is no creature hidden from His sight, but all things are open and laid bare to the eyes of Him with Whom we are accountable." (Hebrews 4:13)**

All of earth's inhabitants will someday stand before God at the judgment seat of Christ and will have to give an account for the one life that He gave them breath for. This will be the final and permanent shift to biblical reality where the Word of God will be the measuring tool. God will ask every person if he accomplished the task that He had designated for us to carry out as part of His purposes on earth. We will not even have to answer because our works that were done according to God's will shall be supernaturally be seen by all. **"For we must all appear before the judgment seat of Christ, that each one may be recompensed for his deeds in the body, according to what he has done, whether good or bad." (2 Corinthians 5:10)** This will be good news for those who have chosen to believe and serve Christ now in the hopes of His rewards for them later. But for those who have chosen to live by Jack Canfield's success principles, planning their whole life around earning money and going on vacations, this scene will be to their utter horror. They will find out that they chose the wrong world to be successful in. Let us use discernment while we can and not make this catastrophic mistake.

This Is Only A Test

CHAPTER TWELVE

In the beginning, there were two trees in the Garden. The tree of life was there to avail eternal life to people, but the tree of the knowledge of good and evil was also there with fruit bursting full of false promises. God gave man a free will to choose and He still give us that choice today, knowing that godless self-will autonomy carries heavy consequences.

Faith, trust and belief are not activated until they are challenged and tested. Anyone can say that they believe in something or someone, but it is not valid and does not come alive until a life circumstance puts that trust to the test. If a person remains true to what he says he believes after the Word of God is challenged, then he really believes. Just like Adam and Eve, our belief in God is tried and tested by the availability of false teaching.

We can see from reviewing these world views that there are only two ways that man can live: either as a proud, stubborn, self-god or as a humble, innocent, dependent child of God. We will either rely on self-will power and the spirits of the age or we will find Christ and rely on His Holy Spirit to fill us, enlighten us and quicken us with the power to live by the truth. Our choice will be to either do whatever it takes to get by, operating on evil wisdom, or discover godly discernment and live by faith in the holy wisdom of God. We will either live in the sham of a shadow of glory, treasure hunting and mining for earth's gold or set our hearts on treasure stored up for us in Heaven and be willing to believe for all that God has waiting for us. We will either follow our dark loves and the sinful pleasures of our darkest desires or we will rise above the grip of depravity and give our heart to the true lover of our souls who washes us clean from the filth of sin. The stage is set for us to follow our hearts and choose our true love.

I will finish with a story from the Old Testament about a young man named Daniel who made godly choices from his youth and how God came to his side when he was put to the test. Daniel was among the sons of Israel's nobility who were captured by the Chaldeans and taken away to live in Babylon in service to the enemy king. Daniel underwent the teaching and training in the knowledge, literature and ways of this pagan culture. But through his Jewish heritage, Daniel had given his heart to the God of Israel whom he knew to be the true God. Daniel was resolved that, no matter how much false teaching and brain washing he was made to endure, he would not forsake his commitment to the God of Heaven. In response to his faithfulness, God gave Daniel supernatural wisdom, opened his mind with godly discernment and gave him the ability to interpret dreams and visions. In fact, God gave Daniel wisdom that was ten times better than all the magicians of the king's court.

One night, King Nebuchadnezzar had a troubling dream and he called for all of his magicians and sorcerers to stand before him to tell him the dream along with the interpretation so that he would know if they were telling him the truth. These men were highly trained in the occultic arts. They were probably very accomplished in meditation, visualization, channeling and other ways to contact demonic powers for secret knowledge. Even so, they were at a loss because they could not produce the answers that the king was looking for.

The king became enraged because none of his so-called wise men had the wisdom to disclose the dream and its interpretation according to what he had required. Therefore, he ordered all them to be slain, including Daniel and his fellow captives. Daniel went before the king and asked that the court magicians and sorcerers not be killed. He would consult the God of Heaven who knows all things to give him the information that the king had asked.

Daniel sought God through prayer and God answered him by telling him the dream and the interpretation. **"Then the mystery was revealed to Daniel in a night vision. Then Daniel blessed the God of Heaven." (Daniel 2:19)** Daniel was able to go before the king of Babylon and tell him the mysteries that God had shown him. The king confirmed that Daniel had told him the truth. The lives of the king's wise men were spared and this Chaldean king worshiped the God of Heaven because of the supernatural wisdom that the Lord had given his servant Daniel. His message brought full understanding and belief to this pagan king's heart. **"The king answered Daniel and said, 'Surely your God is a God of gods and a Lord of kings and a revealer of mysteries, since you have been able to reveal this mystery.'" (Daniel 2:47)**

The king promoted Daniel to be chief over all wise men in Babylon. All this happened because, when it came to the test, Daniel fully trusted the God of Heaven and stepped on stage into the limelight to bring about God's purposes. The light of truth cut through the mystery of the unknown and truth had its day. The God of Heaven was glorified by this encounter. Through faith in the true God, Daniel surpassed all those who practiced their secret occultic arts. They were no match for godly wisdom. They could only stand back and be amazed by the accuracy of it.

We can see from this story that the wisdom that God offers far surpasses any knowledge that this world or underworld has to offer. It is better to trust and obey God than to believe that there is some other wisdom that is better, more exciting and more beneficial. We cannot take the shortcut by circumventing God and trusting in self to obtain knowledge.

Because Daniel was faithful in using his gift of discernment, God was able to allow him to see the end of time through a vision, writing it down to warn mankind of ungodly princes that would arise upon the earth to lead people astray. God does not give people the ability to see pictures in their minds so that we can fantasize and visualize what we want for ourselves. He gives us this ability so that He can communicate messages to us in the full "language" of the Spirit which includes dreams and visions. As we can see from this passage in the Bible, these visions were to express God's redemptive purposes on earth, drawing the nations to Himself. He gives us glimpses of His plans in Heaven so that we can pray, announce and move in faith to bring those God-sized, God-centered activities into the earth. Daniel stepped on stage at just the right time in history to stop judgment, and bring God's revelation and mercy to those who were formerly deceived. With godly discernment, we can do the same thing.

"All the world's a stage, and all the men and women are merely players..." How then will we live as players of Heaven's purposes upon the earth? What part will we play to be used by God in our culture? As He equips us to do his will, let us trust the God of Heaven who gives us supernatural spiritual discernment and exhibit our belief in Him in the days ahead.

Prayer To Receive Jesus Christ As Lord And Savior

Dear Jesus,

As I read this book, I understand that I am a sinner before You. I want to give up my sin and turn to You. I want to live for You and have everything that You have planned for me.

I believe that You are the Son of God. I believe that You came to earth and lived as a Man. You were crucified on a cross and there You bore the punishment of my sin. I believe that You rose from the dead on the third day. I believe that You now stand at the right hand of the Father on my behalf in Heaven. I ask You to forgive me of my sin and selfishness and ask You to take full control of me. Help me to live a life that is pleasing to God now and forever. Amen.

"If we confess our sins, He is faithful and just to forgive us our sins and to cleanse us from all unrighteousness. If we say that we have not sinned, we make Him a liar, and His word is not in us." (1 John 1:9-10)

THE EVIL OF TRUSTING IN YOURSELF AND TRUSTING IN WEALTH

Proverbs 28:11 "The rich man is wise in his own eyes, but the poor who has understanding sees through him."

Proverbs 28:26 "He who trusts in his own heart is a fool, but he who walks wisely will be delivered."

Psalms 52:3-7 "You love evil more than good, falsehood more than speaking what is right. You love all words that devour, O deceitful tongue. But God will break you down forever, He will snatch you up, and tear you away from your tent, and uproot you from the land of the living. Selah. And the righteous will see and fear; and will laugh at him, saying 'Behold, the man who would not make God his refuge, but trusted in the abundance of his riches, and was strong in his evil desire.'"

Psalms 53:1 "The fool has said in his heart, 'There is no God,' They are corrupt, and have committed abominable injustice; There is no one who does good."

Ezekiel 7:19 "They shall fling their silver into the streets, and their gold shall become an abhorrent thing; their silver and their gold shall not be able to deliver them in the day of the wrath of the Lord."

James 1:9-11 "But let the brother of humble circumstances glory in his high position; and let the rich man glory in his humiliation, because like flowering grass he will pass away. For the sun rises with a scorching wind, and withers the grass; and its flower falls off, and the beauty of its appearance is destroyed; so too the rich man in the midst of his pursuits will fade away."

James 5: 1-3 "Come now, you rich, weep and howl for your miseries which are coming upon you. Your riches have rotted and your garments have become moth-eaten. Your gold and your silver have rusted; and their rust will be a witness against you and will consume your flesh like fire. It is in the last days that you have stored up your treasure!"

Matthew 6:19,21 "Do not lay up for yourselves treasures upon earth, where moth and rust destroy, and where thieves break in and steal…for where your treasure is, there will your heart be also."

Habakkuk 2:4-5 "Look at the proud! Their spirit is not right in them, but the righteous live by their faith. Moreover, wealth is treacherous; the arrogant do not endure. They open their throats wide as Sheol; like death they never have enough."

TRUSTING IN GOD ALONE

Habakkuk 3:19 "God, the Lord, is my strength; he makes my feet like the feet of a deer, and makes me tread upon the heights."

James 5:8 "You too be patient; strengthen your hearts, for the coming of the Lord is at hand."

Ephesians 6:10-11 "Finally, be strong in the Lord, and in the strength of His might. Put on the full armor of God, that you may be able to stand firm against the schemes of the devil."

Colossians 2:6-7 "As you therefore have received Christ Jesus the Lord, so walk in Him, having been firmly rooted and now being built up in Him and established in your faith, just as you were instructed, and overflowing with gratitude."

Colossians 3:1-2 "If then you have been raised up with Christ, keep seeking the things above, where Christ is, seated at the right hand of God. Set your mind on the things above, not on the things that are on earth."

2 Peter 1:2-3 "Grace and peace be multiplied to you in the knowledge of God and of Jesus our Lord; seeing that His divine power has granted to us everything pertaining to life and godliness, through the true knowledge of Him who called us by His own glory and excellence."

2 Peter 3:9 "The Lord is not slow about His promise, as some count slowness, but is patient toward you, not wishing for any to perish but for all to come to repentance."

1 Peter 1:3-5 "Blessed be the God and Father of our Lord Jesus Christ, who according to His great mercy has caused us to be born again to a living hope through the resurrection of Jesus Christ from the dead, to obtain an inheritance which is imperishable and undefiled and will not fade away, reserved in heaven for you, who are protected by the power of God through faith for a salvation ready to be revealed in the last time."

1 Peter 2:25 "For you were continually straying like sheep, but now you have returned to the Shepherd and Guardian of your souls."

Hebrews 11:24-27 "By faith, Moses, when he had grown up, refused to be called the son of Pharaoh's daughter; choosing rather to endure ill-treatment with the people of God, than to enjoy the passing pleasures of sin; considering the reproach of Christ greater riches than the treasures of Egypt; for he was looking to the reward. By faith he left Egypt, not fearing the wrath of the king; for he endured, as seeing Him who is unseen."

1 Corinthians 2:4-5 "And my message and my preaching were not in persuasive words of wisdom, but in demonstration of the Spirit and of power, that your faith should not rest on the wisdom of men, but on the power of God."

Philippians 3:2-3 "Beware of the dogs, beware of the evil workers, beware of the false circumcision; for we are the true circumcision, who worship in the Spirit of God and glory in Christ Jesus and put no confidence in the flesh…"

Philippians 3:7 "But whatever things were gain to me, those things I have counted as loss for the sake of Christ."

Psalms 86: 8-10 "There is no one like Thee among the gods, O Lord; Nor are there any works like Thine. All nations whom Thou hast made shall come and worship before Thee, O Lord; And they shall glorify Thy name. For Thou are great and doest wondrous deeds; Thou alone are God."

Psalms 115: 9-11 "O Israel, trust in the Lord; He is their help and their shield. O house of Aaron, trust in the Lord; He is their help and their shield. You who fear the Lord, trust in the Lord; He is their help and their shield."

Psalms 121: 1-2 "I will lift up my eyes to the mountains; from whence shall my help come from? My help comes from the Lord, who made heaven and earth."

Psalms 121: 7-8 "The Lord will protect you from all evil; The Lord will guard your going out and your coming in from this time forth and forevermore."

WARNINGS OF FALSE TEACHERS

1 John 4:1 "Beloved, do not believe every spirit, but test the spirits to see whether they are from God; because many false prophets have gone out into the world."

Proverbs 28:10 "He who leads the upright astray in an evil way will himself fall into his own pit, but the blameless will inherit good."

1 Corinthians 10:21 "You cannot drink the cup of the Lord and the cup of demons; you cannot partake of the table of the Lord and the table of demons."

Philippians 3: 17-19 "Brethren, join in following my example, and observe those who walk according to the pattern you have in us. For many walk, of whom I often told you, and now tell you even weeping, that they are enemies of the cross of Christ, whose end is destruction, whose god is their appetite, and whose glory is in their shame, who set their minds on earthly things."

2 Peter 1:16 "For we did not follow cleverly devised tales when we made known to you the power and coming of our Lord Jesus Christ, but we were eyewitnesses of His majesty."

2 Peter 2:1-3 "But false prophets also arose among the people, just as there will also be false teachers among you, who will secretly introduce destructive heresies, even denying the Master who bought them, bring swift destruction upon themselves. And many will follow their sensuality, and because of them the way of the truth will be maligned; and in their greed they will exploit you with false words…"

2 Peter 2:17-18 "You therefore, beloved, since you are forewarned, beware that you are not carried away with the error of the lawless and lose your own stability. But grow in the grace and knowledge of our Lord and Savior Jesus Christ."

1 Corinthians 10: 19-20 "What do I mean then? That a thing sacrificed to idols is anything, or that an idol is anything? No, but I say that the things which the Gentiles sacrifice, they sacrifice to demons, and not to God; and I do not want you to become sharers in demons."

Jude:8 "Yet in the same manner, these men, also by dreaming, defile the flesh, and reject authority, and revile angelic majesties."

Daniel 11:32 "And by smooth words he will turn to godlessness those who act wickedly toward the covenant, but the people who know their God will display strength and take action."

2 Thessalonians 2:3-4 "Let no one in any way deceive you, for it will not come unless the apostasy comes first, and the man of lawlessness is revealed, the son of destruction, who opposes and exalts himself above every so-called god or object of worship, so that he takes his seat in the temple of God, displaying himself as being God."

1 John 2:15 "Do not love the world, nor the things in the world. If anyone loves the world, the love of the Father is not in him."

1 John 2:18 "Children, it is the last hour; and just as you heard that antichrist is coming, even now many antichrists have arisen; from this we know that it is the last hour."

1 John 2:22 "Who is the liar but the one who denies that Jesus is the Christ? This is the antichrist, and the one who denies the Father and the Son."

Hebrews 13:9 "Do not be carried away by all kinds of strange teachings."

WARNING OF COMING JUDGMENT

1 Thessalonians 5:3-4 "While they are saying, 'Peace and safety!' then destruction will come upon them suddenly like birth pangs upon a woman with child; and they shall not escape. But you, brethren, are not in darkness, that the day should overtake you like a thief..."

2 Thessalonians 2:11-12 "And for this reason God will send upon them a deluding influence so that they might believe what is false, in order that they all may be judged who did not believe the truth, but took pleasure in wickedness."

James 1:14-16 "But each one is tempted when he is carried away and enticed by his own lust. Then when lust has conceived, it gives birth to sin; and when sin is accomplished, it brings forth death."

1 Peter 4:3-5 "For the time already past is sufficient for you to have carried out the desire of the Gentiles, having pursued a course of sensuality, lusts, drunkenness, carousals, drinking parties and abominable idolatries. And in all this, they are surprised that you do not run with them into the same excess of dissipation, and they malign you; but they shall give account to Him who is ready to judge the living and the dead"

John 3:20-21 "For everyone who does evil hates the light, and does not come to the light, lest his deeds should be exposed. But he who practices the truth comes to the light, that his deeds may be manifested as having been wrought in God."

2 Peter 3:7 "But the present heavens and earth by His word are being reserved for fire, kept for the day of judgment and destruction of ungodly men."

Jude: 14-15 "And about these also Enoch, in the seventh generation from Adam, prophesied, saying, 'Behold, the Lord came with many thousands of His holy ones, to execute judgment upon all, and to convict all the ungodly of all their ungodly deeds which they have done in an ungodly way, and of all the harsh things which ungodly sinners have spoken against Him."

DISCERNMENT

Proverbs 28:5 "Evil men do not understand justice, but those who seek the Lord understand all things."

Daniel 1:17 "And as for these four youths, God gave them knowledge and intelligence in every branch of literature and wisdom; Daniel even understood all kinds of visions and dreams."

Daniel 1:20 "And as for every matter of wisdom and understanding about which the king consulted them, he found them ten times better than all the magicians and conjurers who were in all his realm."

Daniel 2:20-22 "Daniel answered and said, 'Let the name of God be blessed forever and ever, for wisdom and power belong to Him. And it is He who changes the times and the epochs; He removes kings and establishes kings; He gives wisdom to wise men, and knowledge to men of understanding. It is He who reveals the profound and hidden things; He knows what is in the darkness, and the light dwells with Him."

Matthew 16:15-17 "He said to them, 'But who do you say that I am?' And Simon Peter answered and said, 'Thou art the Christ, the Son of the living God.' And Jesus answered and said to him, 'Blessed are you, Simon Barjona, because flesh and blood did not reveal this to you, but My Father who is in heaven."

Philippians 1:9-10 "And this I pray, that your love may abound still more and more in real knowledge and all discernment, so that you may approve the things that are excellent, in order to be sincere and blameless until the day of Christ…"

Hebrews 11:27 "By faith he left Egypt, not fearing the wrath of the king; for he endured, as seeing Him who is unseen."

THE WORD OF GOD

Proverbs 28:7 "He who keeps the law is a discerning son…"

Psalm 86:11 "Teach me Thy way, O Lord; I will walk in Thy truth…"

Psalm 119:18 "Open my eyes, that I may behold wonderful things from Thy law."

Psalm 119: 14-16 "I have rejoiced in the way of Thy testimonies, as much as in all riches. I will meditate on Thy precepts and regard Thy ways. I shall delight in Thy statutes; I shall not forget Thy word."

Psalm 119:27 "Make me understand the way of Thy precepts, so I will meditate on Thy wonders."

Psalm 119:29 "Remove the false way from me, and graciously grant me Thy law."

Psalm 119:163 "I hate and despise falsehood, but I love Thy law."

John 8:31-32 "Jesus therefore was saying to those Jews who had believed Him, 'If you abide in My word, then you are truly disciples of Mine; and you shall know the truth, and the truth shall make you free.'"

Isaiah 51:4 "Pay attention to Me, O My people; and give ear to Me, O My nation; for a law will go forth from Me, and I will set My justice for a light of the peoples."

1 Peter 1:22-23 "Since you have in obedience to the truth purified your souls for a sincere love of the brethren, fervently love one another from the heart, for you have been born again not of seed which is perishable but imperishable, that is, through the living and abiding word of God."

1 Peter 1:24-25 "For, 'All flesh is like grass, and all its glory like the flower of grass, the grass withers, and the flower falls off, but the word of the Lord abides forever.' And this is the word which was preached to you."

GOD OUR CREATOR

Psalm 86:9-10 "All nations whom Thou hast made shall come and worship before Thee, O Lord; and they shall glorify Thy name. For Thou art great and doest wondrous deeds; Thou alone art God.

Isaiah 41:20 "That they may see and recognize, and consider and gain insight as well, that the hand of the Lord has done this, and the Holy One of Israel has created it."

Ezekiel 18:4 "Behold, all souls are Mine; the soul of the father as well as the soul of the son is Mine."

Ezekiel 44:28 "And it shall be with regard to an inheritance for them, that I am their inheritance; and you shall give them no possession in Israel—I am their possession."

1 Corinthians 4:20 "For the kingdom of God does not consist in words, but in power."

Hebrews 13:8 "Jesus Christ is the same yesterday and today, yes and forever."

1 John 3:8 "The Son of God appeared for this purpose, that He might destroy the works of the devil."

ETERNAL LIFE AND THE NEW EARTH

Mark 13:31 "Heaven and earth will pass away, but My words will not pass away."

John 14:1-2 "Let not your heart be troubled; believe in God, believe also in Me. In My Father's house are many dwelling places; if it were not so, I would have told you; for I go to prepare a place for you."

Hebrews 11:16 "But as it is, they desire a better country, that is a heavenly one. Therefore God is not ashamed to be called their God; for He has prepared a city for them."

Hebrews 13:14 For here we do not have a lasting city, but we are seeking the city which is to come."

2 Peter 3:11-13 "Since all these things are to be destroyed in this way, what sort of people ought you to be in holy conduct and godliness, looking for and hastening the coming of the day of God, on account of which the heavens will be destroyed by burning, and the elements will melt with intense heat! But according to His promise we are looking for a new heavens and a new earth, in which righteousness dwells."

1 John 2:25 "And this is the promise which He Himself made to us: eternal life."

References

Byrne, Rhonda, *The Secret*, Beyond Words Publishing, Hillsboro, 2006

Canfield, Jack and Hansen, Mark Victor, *Chicken Soup For The Soul*, Health Communications, Inc., Deerfield Beach, 1993

Canfield, Jack and Hansen, Mark Victor, *A 2nd Helping Of Chicken Soup For The Soul*, Health Communications, Inc., Deerfield Beach, 1995

Canfield, Jack and Hansen, Mark Victor, *Chicken Soup For The Soul: Living Your Dreams*, Health Communications, Inc., Deerfield Beach, 2003

Canfield, Jack and Hansen, Mark Victor, *Chicken Soup For The Christian Soul*, Health Communications, Inc., Deerfield Beach, 2004

Canfield, Jack, *The Success Principles*, HarperCollins Publishers, New York, 2005

Carlson, Ron and Decker, Ed, *Fast Facts on False Teachings*, Harvest House Publishers, Eugene, 1994

Colson, Chuck, *How Now Shall We Live?*, Tyndale House Publishers, Inc., Wheaton, 1999

Davich, Victor N., *The Best Guide To Meditation*, Renaissance Media, New York, 1998

Flood, Gavin, *An Introduction To Hinduism*, Cambridge University Press, Cambridge, 1996

Feurstein, Georg, *The Deeper Dimension Of Yoga*, Shambhala Publications, Inc., Boston, 2003

Gawain, Shakti, *Creative Visualization*, Nataraj Publishing, Novato, 2002

Gawain, Shakti, *Return To The Garden*, New World Library, San Rafael, 1989

Guiley, Rosemary Ellen, *Harper's Encyclopedia Of Mystical & Paranormal Experience*, HarperCollins Publishers, Inc., New York, 1991

Hill, Napoleon, *Think And Grow Rich*, Penguin Group, New York, 2003

Hodge, Bodie, *The Fall Of Satan*, New Leaf Publishing Group, Green Forest, 2011

Hunt, Dave, *Seeking And Finding God*, The Berean Call, Bend, 2004

Hunt, Dave, *The Cult Explosion*, Harvest House Publishers, Eugene, 1980

REFERENCES

Hunt, Dave, *Yoga And The Body Of Christ*, The Berean Call, Bend, 2006

Mason, Paul, *The Maharishi*, Element Books Ltd., Shaftesbury, 1994

McDowell, Josh and Stewart, Don, *Understanding Secular Religions*, Here's Life Publishers, Inc., San Bernardino, 1982

Noebel, David A., *The Battle For Truth*, Harvest House Publishers, Eugene, 2001

Shakespeare, William, *As You Like It*

Schaeffer, Francis A., *How Should We Then Live?*, Crossway Books, Wheaton, 1983

Webber, Andrew Lloyd, *The Phantom Of The Opera*

Webster, Richard, *Creative Visualization For Beginners*, Llewellyn Publications, Woodbury, 2005

Wright, Machaelle Small, *Behaving As If The God In All Life Mattered*, Perelandra, Ltd., Warrenton, 1983

Yogi, Maharishi Mahesh, *Transcendental Meditation*, Allied Publishers Private Limited, London, 1963

Yogi, Maharishi Mahesh, *Science Of Being And Art Of Living: Transcendental Meditation*, Penguin Group, New York, 1963

Made in the USA
Charleston, SC
21 January 2012